The Dreamer's
DICTIONARY

Unlocking your dreams using Biblical Truths

ELIZABETH A. WEBER

ACKNOWLEDGMENTS

All glory and praise to my Lord Jesus Christ, who is the author and finisher of my faith.
All credit is due Him who strengthened me to finish this enormous project, and it is by His strength, wisdom, knowledge, and understanding that He has made this book possible.

This book is dedicated to my wonderful and encouraging husband, Steve, and to my beautiful children, Brooke, Billy, and Isaiah. I love you!

Thank you to the countless volunteers who freely gave of their time and energy editing and helping in the preparation of this book: Debbie, Carmen, my parents, Roger and Lolly, Pastor Steve and Ginny, Sharon and Kelly. This would not have been possible without you.

CONTENTS

FOREWORD

E verybody dreams. I feel fairly safe in making that statement. In my past personal experience I would have to say that I usually forgot most of my dreams. I would wake up with some awareness that I had dreamed, but the details were fuzzy at best. I would put the dream aside and then forget about it. However, there are those times when our dreams are vivid and every detail seems to jump out. In those times you might even sense in your spirit that it is significant. But where do you go from there? Scripture clearly tells us that God speaks to us through dreams.

I am so blessed that my good friend Elizabeth Weber has a God-given gift of dream interpretation. Elizabeth is a solid Christian, not given to extremes. Her gift is truly trustworthy. Not only has Elizabeth been blessed with dream interpretation, but in her book she shares the principles and scriptures that can stir others to their own understanding of dream interpretation.

I must confess that understanding my dreams—unless they were so completely unforgettable—was not high on my list of priorities. I have since needed to repent of that attitude. God speaks to us through dreams, still today. To open yet another avenue of revelation that is biblical is exciting. Nothing can be more powerful than a word from our Lord.

This book, I believe, will open your spirit to powerful and fresh communication with the gracious Holy Spirit. I encourage you to pursue discipleship by the Spirit of God. This book is a practical resource that enables the dreamer to know and understand their dreams and visions.

Pastor Stephen McPherson
City Center Foursquare Church
Redmond, Oregon

INTRODUCTION

In pursuit of the interpretation of my own dreams, I have found that reliable tools, founded upon God's Word, are difficult to find. Although some prove to be valuable, many are based upon theory and speculation rather than biblical truth. There are plenty of dream interpretation guides to be found on the Internet and in the libraries, but most of them are based upon counterfeit ideals.

After much frustrating research, I found the only true and reliable resources to interpret my dreams and visions to be the Bible, a Bible dictionary, Webster's dictionary and thesaurus, a Bible encyclopedia, and *Strong's Exhaustive Concordance*. These, along with the help of the Holy Spirit, became the only reference tools and resources I needed in writing this book, and I will never go outside of these resources again.

After narrowing my resources, I was still frustrated with the armload of books that were needed for interpreting my dreams. I had to pull them out of the bookshelf, haul them downstairs to the table, and search through them one at a time, sometimes more than twice to interpret the words and themes in my dreams. Believe it or not, I can't tell you how many times I strained my wrist and elbow from picking up the concordance and Bible dictionaries. My only thought at the time was, *It would be so much easier if I could put all these books into one easy reference guide. What a great idea.* Little did I know the amount of time and the huge commitment it would take to make this book available. But the joy of having it at my fingertips is now a great reward. Although it is not an exhaustive reference of every possible subject in dreams, it covers most of the dreams I've interpreted so far in my own life and in my ministry.

Many of us tend to believe that we're unable to interpret our own dreams. Rather than pursuing the answers for ourselves in God's Word, we seek the help of other "dream interpreters" before we seek the Lord for His counsel. There is a place for seeking counsel. In fact, the Word says:

> *A wise man will hear and increase learning, and a man of understanding will attain wise counsel, to understand a proverb and an enigma, the words of the wise and their riddles.*
>
> *Proverbs 1:5-6 (NKJV)*

A dream is a riddle or a mystery, a proverb or an enigma. He calls people who pursue increased learning of these riddles "wise."

I believe that God wants to raise up gifted dream interpreters, and many people are being saved because of this gift; but, more than that, He wants us to learn to understand His mysterious communications with us in our dreams and visions and begin to find the answers for ourselves before we enlist the help of others. We need to be people who understand the importance of going to the Scriptures when looking for answers to these questions and asking what these symbols mean according to the Bible. We need to understand how Jesus speaks in parables and begin to use the right "process of interpretation" when interpreting these dreams and visions. God wants to speak to us, but we must pursue His voice with all our heart.

This book is for anyone who dreams and wants to seek out the mystery of their dream or vision in light of what God might be saying to them. Limiting the audience to a group of Christians would be limiting God's ability to bring light to the world. This book is intended to help the entire saved or unsaved community that wants answers for the "stirrings in the night." This could include individuals ranging from the satanic community to the Pentecostal crowd. If someone is seeking answers, I want them to feel that my book might be an appropriate and helpful place to start, and from there I hope my words will direct them to the Bible and to God.

My hope in writing this book is to inspire you to listen to your dreams and visions and to begin to understand what God is telling you by using the right tools and resources. My intent is not to develop dream interpreters of other people's dreams, but to help each person understand and interpret their own dreams and visions and the ways that God is speaking to them. This book is a great tool, but the ultimate tool is the Bible itself.

CHAPTER 1

WHERE DO DREAMS AND VISIONS COME FROM?

The Bible says that dreams and visions are but a couple of the ways that God speaks to His people.

In a dream, in a vision of the night, when deep sleep falls upon men, while slumbering on their beds, then He opens the ears of men, and seals their instructions. In order to turn man from his deeds, and conceal pride from man, He keeps back his soul from the Pit, and his life from perishing by the sword.

Job 33:15-18

Then He said, "Hear now My words: If there is a prophet among you, I, the Lord, make Myself known to him in a vision; I speak to him in a dream."

Numbers 12:6

Not all dreams are from God, and not all dreams that we may call "nightmares" are from the devil. Sometimes the Lord has to shake us up and go to extremes to get our attention. God gave Job a dream that brought him to a place of fear and trembling, but this dream was definitely from the Lord.

Now a word was secretly brought to me, and my ear received a whisper of it. In disquieting thoughts from the visions of the night, when deep sleep falls on me, fear came upon me, and trembling, which made all my bones shake.

Job 4:12-14

Nebuchadnezzar had dreams that troubled him greatly, but God revealed their mystery to Daniel, who interpreted them for him. These dreams were definitely from the Lord.

Now in the second year of Nebuchadnezzar's reign, Nebuchadnezzar had dreams; and his spirit was so troubled that his sleep left him.

Daniel 2:1

Pilate's wife also had a dream that caused her much suffering. The fact that she acted upon the dream shows that she believed the warning was from the Lord:

While he was sitting on the judgment seat, his wife sent to him, saying, "Have nothing to do with that just Man, for I have suffered many things today in a dream because of Him."

Matthew 27:19

Job knew very well that God was capable of getting his attention through his dreams and visions. It's clear that Job was speaking to the Lord when he said:

Then you scare me with dreams and terrify me with visions so that my soul chooses strangling and death rather than my body.

Job 7:14-15

Most of us have experienced a nightmare at some point in our life. I've personally had dreams of death, rape, and even being chased by a bear, but many of these nightmares turned out to be promptings from the Lord to intercede in a situation or even to warn me of coming events. It's important that we pay close attention to every dream we have. It would be a shame to miss out on a word of communication from the Lord simply because we don't like what the dream is about. We need to take every dream seriously until it has been tested with the Word of God and His Holy Spirit. Many times people are drawn to the Lord as a result of seeking an interpretation for a nightmare.

The world is seeking out answers for their dreams from worldly psychics, sorcerers, and mediums, and we must begin to bring the truth to the streets and to the marketplace. If we don't get the dream interpreters out on the streets, then the lost will seek the counsel of the world for their dreams and remain lost. The good news is that the face of evangelism is beginning to change. It's exciting to see Christ-based dream interpretation tables being set up in county fairs, marketplaces, and street corners, making the truth available to the world. Many are being saved through the interpretation of their dreams. When they understand that God is speaking to them in their own dreams they realize that He loves them, knows them, and is calling them to Himself. When they hear the true interpretation, it leaves a seed of truth in their heart and very often opens wide the door to share the gospel of Christ with them.

So where do our dreams come from? Dreams can come from several sources. They can come from:

- God
- Our own soul (soul dreams)
- Demonic influences or the devil
- Physical illness
- Induced medication (drugs) or alcohol

You might ask, "What is a 'soul' dream?" The soul is made up of the mind, will, and emotions. Soulish dreams involve these aspects of our character having been stirred by our own fleshly desires. What we think about or focus on during the day can influence what we dream about at night. If our mind is focused on soulish things during the day, we can fall prey to soulish dreams at night. We can literally cause ourselves to dream about certain things. If we aren't tuned in to the Holy Spirit and have not submitted our personal desires to God, then we can be subjected to dreams from our mind, will, or emotions.

> *For thus says the Lord of hosts, the God of Israel: Do not let your prophets and your diviners who are in your midst deceive you, nor listen to your dreams which you cause to be dreamed.*
>
> *Jeremiah 29:8*

Our dreams reveal the secrets of our heart even though our conscious minds may not be aware of them. Our dreams will very often reveal those secrets to us through the Holy Spirit.

> *For what man knows the things of a man except the spirit of the man which is in him? Even so no one knows the things of God except the Spirit of God.*
>
> *1 Corinthians 2:11*

DOES GOD COMMUNICATE WITH US IN DREAMS AND VISIONS?

Many times I've found myself running after the prophets of this age, hoping for the chance of hearing a word of direction or encouragement from the Lord. I've traveled many miles, seeking a prophetic word from God, and sometimes found that I've subjected myself to counterfeit means. I've also spent much time dwelling in a spiritual desert or valley longer than needed, simply because I haven't listened or paid attention to my own dreams or visions. So many of us are ignorant of the fact that God is speaking directly to us in the night seasons.

> *I will bless the Lord who has given me counsel; my heart also instructs me in the night seasons.*
>
> *Psalm 16:7*

If we would simply realize that many of our dreams and visions are coming to us directly from the Lord, our pursuit after His voice would not take us so far from His plan. The time spent running after a prophetic word from God could so easily be minimized if we would simply seek His face and His Word with all our heart and tune our ear to His voice.

In a dream, in a vision of the night, when deep sleep falls upon men, while slumbering on their beds, then He opens the ears of men, and seals their instruction. In order to turn man from his deed, and conceal pride from man, He keeps back his soul from the Pit, and his life from perishing by the sword.

Job 33:14-18

God knows who we are, what our concerns are, and what we need to hear. It's unfathomable to realize nearly everyone has dreams in the night seasons, and every dream is different and specific to our own life situations. The expanse and greatness of God and His wisdom leaves me in awe of His love and mercy for us. He loves each and every one of us and cares deeply for our needs. He simply wants us to pay attention to His voice and believe that He wants to speak to us.

And it shall come to pass afterward that I will pour out My Spirit on all flesh; Your sons and your daughters shall prophesy, your old men shall dream dreams, your young men shall see visions. And also on My menservants and on My maidservants I will pour out My Spirit in those days.

Joel 2:28-29

Probably the greatest evidence that God is still speaking to us in dreams and visions in these days is the passage of Scripture in Acts 2 where the words of Joel, the prophet, are repeated:

And it shall come to pass in the last days, says God, that I will pour out of My Spirit on all flesh; Your sons and your daughters shall prophesy, your young men shall see visions, your old men shall dream dreams. And on My menservants and on my maidservants I will pour out My Spirit in those days.

Acts 2:17-18

This passage of Scripture was clearly written after the death and resurrection of Jesus Christ and was spoken by Peter on the day of Pentecost when the Holy Spirit had come and rested upon man. The question one might ask is, Are we in the last days? My answer to you would be this: Was the Holy Spirit poured out? Obviously, yes. Therefore, we must be in the last days.

There are some who believe "the last days" refers to something they call the "apostolic age." They believe this prophecy of Joel was fulfilled on the day of Pentecost and that Peter stood up to explain to those assembled in the room exactly what they were witnessing and experiencing. There is a problem with this theory.

Prophetic words were given all through the Old and New Testaments, and each time a prophetic word was fulfilled, God made sure there was testimony of that fulfillment in Scripture. Even the words concerning the coming of Christ in the Old Testament were later confirmed in the Gospels, which outlined their fulfillment. If the prophetic word given in Acts 2:17-18 was for the "apostolic age," we would have seen these things testified about in Scripture, and there would have been an account of their fulfillment. God would not have let His testimony of their fulfillment be left out of His Word. The fact remains that we never heard testimony in the New Testament about sons and daughters prophesying, of old men dreaming dreams, or of young men seeing visions. There was no testimony of the sun or moon turning to blood or great signs in the heavens and the earth beneath. These things did not happen in what some call the "apostolic age." Therefore it is clear to me that this prophecy is for the last days when Christ comes, or as it says, "before the coming of the great and awesome day of the Lord."

It also says that God will pour out His Spirit on "all" flesh. Isn't it interesting that dreams are given to both righteous and wicked men? How often do you hear people of all walks of life talk about their dreams? Pharaoh was a wicked man, and he was given a dream that would change the lives of all the people in his earthly kingdom. The Lord gave that dream to Pharaoh. Pharaoh pursued the interpretation, took it to heart, and because of it he was blessed through God's servant, Joseph. That dream also brought about the fulfillment of Joseph's dream about his family.

There are many Christians today who believe God no longer speaks to us in dreams and visions. They believe the only reason God gave people dreams and visions prior to Jesus' death was because they didn't have access to the Scriptures to give them direction. Therefore, since we have the Bible at our fingertips today, God no longer needs to speak to us through dreams and visions. Thankfully, there is much evidence in the Word that God spoke in dreams and visions even after much of the New Testament was written. Three of the Gospels (Matthew, Mark, and Luke), along with Ephesians, Colossians, Philippians, and Philemon, were already written before the dreams and visions were even given to the apostle John concerning the book of Revelation.

The Bible also says that God is the same yesterday, today, and forever (Hebrews 13:8). He has not changed and never will change. We need to stand on that promise in all circumstances and not question it. His promises are yes and amen. His communication with us has remained and will remain the same until we go home to be with Him.

It is a fact that the Lord used dreams and visions in the Bible over two hundred times, and many of the most significant events transpired because of a dream or a vision. Here are a few examples:

DREAMS IN THE BIBLE:

1. Joseph had a dream that his brothers would bow down to the earth before him (Genesis 37:5-10).
2. Joseph interpreted the dreams of Pharaoh, which led to his promotion and the fulfillment of God's word in his first dream (Genesis 41).
3. Gideon heard the telling of a dream that the camp of Midian would be given into his hands (Judges 7:13-15).

4. Solomon was granted wisdom and understanding to judge his people and to discern between good and evil in a dream (1 Kings 3:5-15).
5. Daniel told Nebuchadnezzar his dream and interpreted it and was promoted in King Nebuchadnezzar's kingdom (Daniel 2 and 4).
6. Daniel was shown the coming judgments of the earth in both dreams and visions (Daniel 7 and 8).
7. Joseph was told in a dream not to be afraid and to take Mary as his wife; he was told that she would bring forth a son, and to call Him Jesus (Matthew 1:20).
8. Joseph was divinely warned in a dream not to return to Herod, but to flee to Egypt. He and his family stayed there until the death of Herod. Another prophecy fulfilled: "Out of Egypt I called My Son" (Matthew 2:12-15).
9. Joseph was told in a dream to move his family to Israel because those who sought to kill Jesus were dead (Matthew 2:19-21).
10. Joseph was told in a dream to move his family to Nazareth, where Jesus grew up (Matthew 2:22-23).
11. Pilate's wife was warned in a dream to have nothing to do with that just man, Jesus (Matthew 27:19).
12. The book of Revelation was given to John by dreams and visions from the Lord (Revelation).

VISIONS IN THE BIBLE:

Visions are like dreams; however, they come to you when you are fully awake and their interpretation is usually much more clear and literal. They are usually more easily understood. Visions are one of the ways that God reveals His plans and purposes to His people.

...the utterance of the man whose eyes are opened, the utterance of him who hears the words of God, who sees the vision of the Almighty, who falls down, with eyes wide open.
Numbers 24:3-4

Here are some examples of visions that were given by the Lord in the Bible:

1. Abram was told in a vision that he would not be childless, but that his descendants would number as the stars (Genesis 15:1-6).
2. The call of Ezekiel was communicated through a vision. He was also given a vision of the future and the new temple (Ezekiel).
3. Daniel was shown in a night vision King Nebuchadnezzar's dream (Daniel 2).
4. Daniel was shown the coming judgments of the earth in both dreams and visions (Daniel 7 and 8).
5. The call of Obadiah was communicated in a vision. He was sent to Edom to tell of their coming judgment (Obadiah).
6. The call of Nahum was communicated in a vision. He was sent to Nineveh to proclaim the coming wrath of the Lord against the city (Nahum).
7. The book of Habakkuk was a vision that transpired between Habakkuk and the Lord (Habakkuk).
8. The women who went looking for Jesus' body at the tomb saw, in a vision, angels proclaiming that He had risen (Luke 24:23).
9. Ananias received a vision that he was to go to Tarsus and lay his hands on Saul (Paul) so that he might receive his sight. Paul received a vision that a man named Ananias would come and lay his hands on him as well (Acts 9:10-12).
10. Peter received a vision concerning his ministry to the Gentiles and the offer given by the Lord for their repentance for eternal life (Acts 11:5-18).
11. Paul was encouraged by a vision to not keep silent in the town of the Corinth, and many were saved and baptized (Acts 18:8-10).
12. The book of Revelation was given to John by dreams and visions from the Lord (Revelation).

The purpose of visions is to lead, guide, and give direction to God's people as well as foretell the future.

PROPHECY THROUGH DREAMS AND VISIONS:

It's clear that God has many ways of revealing His plans to His prophets. One of the greatest accounts of how the Lord communicates with His prophets is shown in the book of Jeremiah. Jeremiah's call was revealed to him in a vision from the Lord. He was shown the judgments that would come against Judah and Jerusalem and was then sent to those people to expose their broken covenant with God and call them to repentance.

> Then said I: "Ah, Lord God! Behold, I cannot speak, for I am a youth."
> But the Lord said to me: "Do not say, 'I am a youth,' for you shall go to all to whom I send you, and whatever I command you, you shall speak. Do not be afraid of their faces, for I am with you to deliver you," says the Lord. Then the Lord put forth His hand and touched my mouth, and the Lord said to me: "Behold, I have put my words in your mouth. See, I have this day set you over the nations and over the kingdoms, to root out and to pull down, to destroy and to throw down, to build and to plant."
> Moreover the word of the Lord came to me, saying, "Jeremiah, what do you see?" And I said, "I see a branch of an almond tree." Then the Lord said to me, "You have seen well, for I am ready to perform My word."
> And the word of the Lord came to me the second time, saying, "What do you see?" And I said, "I see a boiling pot, and it is facing away from the Lord."
> ..."Therefore prepare yourself and arise, and speak to them all that I command you. Do not be dismayed before their faces, lest I dismay you before them."
> Jeremiah 1:6-13,17

Visions and dreams were given to the prophets as a way of communication from God.

Then He said, "Hear now My words: 'If there is a prophet among you, I, the Lord, make Myself known to him in a vision; I speak to him in a dream.'"

Numbers 12:6-7

The prophets' instructions were clear. They were given the dream or vision, sometimes they recorded it, and then they carried it out to an assigned people at an assigned time.

Then the Lord answered me and said: "Write the vision and make it plain on tablets, that he may run who reads it. For the vision is yet for an appointed time; but at the end it will speak, and it will not lie. Though it tarries, wait for it; because it will surely come, it will not tarry."

Habakkuk 2:2-3

Be forewarned that along with every truth and gift given from the Lord, the enemy will seek to deceive people with a counterfeit version of that truth or gift. Just because someone comes to you or to the church saying, "I had a dream," or "The Lord gave me a vision," does not mean that those visions or dreams are from the Lord. Always test the spirits, and line up every word with the Word of God, the Bible (1 John 4:1). It's a dangerous thing to believe the word of a false prophet or false teacher.

And the Lord said to me, "The prophets prophesy lies in My name. I have not sent them, commanded them, nor spoken to them; they prophesy to you a false vision, divination, a worthless thing, and the deceit of their heart. Therefore thus says the Lord concerning the prophets who prophesy in My name, whom I did not send, and who say, 'Sword and famine shall not be in this land; - 'By sword and famine those prophets shall be consumed! And the people to whom they prophesy shall be cast out in the streets of Jerusalem because of the

famine and the sword; they will have no one to bury them
– them nor their wives, their sons nor their daughters – for I
will pour their wickedness on them.'"

Jeremiah 14:14-16

"Behold, I am against the prophets," says the Lord, "who
use their tongues and say, 'He says.' Behold, I am against
those who prophesy false dreams," says the Lord, "and tell
them, and cause My people to err by their lies and by their
recklessness. Yet I did not send them or command them;
therefore they shall not profit this people at all," says the
Lord.

Jeremiah 23:31-32

Keep in mind that God is not against prophets and dreamers,
but against the message of the prophets and dreamers who use their
tongues to prophesy false dreams and lies. He does not warn against
interpreting dreams or visions, or prophecy, but against the message
of false prophets and false interpretations. He is against the false
message which causes people to turn away from God and follow
other gods.

"If there arises among you a prophet or a dreamer of dreams,
and he gives you a sign or a wonder, and the sign or the
wonder comes to pass, of which he spoke to you, saying,
'Let us go after other gods'—which you have not known—
'and let us serve them,' you shall not listen to the words of
that prophet or that dreamer of dreams, for the LORD your
God is testing you to know whether you love the LORD your
God with all your heart and with all your soul. You shall
walk after the LORD your God and fear Him, and keep His
commandments and obey His voice, and you shall serve Him
and hold fast to Him. But that prophet or that dreamer of
dreams shall be put to death, because he has spoken in order
to turn you away from the LORD your God, who brought you
out of the land of Egypt and redeemed you from the house of
bondage, to entice you from the way in which the LORD your

*God commanded you to walk. So you shall put away the evil
from your midst."*

Deuteronomy 13:1-5

You must understand that the devil only counterfeits that which is true. Notice that there are no counterfeit three-dollar bills—because there are no real ones. A counterfeit painting is only a counterfeit if there is a real painting. You can't forge something that doesn't exist. Counterfeit means to copy or imitate something that is real or true in order to deceive. You won't find anywhere in the Bible that the devil wasted time coming up with a new idea. His intention is to use the truth and add a twist. That is why he is trying to deceive people in dream interpretation.

Dream interpretation is an area of study that has long been forgotten, but for some reason the devil feels it's important to counterfeit it again. He probably knows the Bible better than any of us. He knows that in the last days God is going to pour out His Spirit in dreams and visions and prophecy, and that God wants people to know the truth about those dreams and visions. So of course the devil needs to do something about it. Therefore, he must come up with a counterfeit interpretation theology and false interpreters to lead people astray. The fact that false dream interpreters are rising up is a good indication that God is raising up true dream interpreters. The same goes for miracles. The devil will perform a "miracle," which gives him or the man performing the miracle glory rather than God. That is why he poses as an angel of light. He is the great deceiver.

*For such are false apostles, deceitful workers, transforming
themselves into apostles of Christ. And no wonder! For Satan
himself transforms himself into an angel of light. Therefore
it is no great thing if his ministers also transform themselves
into ministers of righteousness, whose end will be according
to their works.*

2 Corinthians 11:13-15

Take warning that God holds you accountable for what you listen to, what you believe, what you say, and what you hear. We must, again, line up every word with the Word of God. Every dream and vision must be interpreted with the evidence of Scripture to back it up. Prophetic dreams, which carry a message of destiny to a people, have a specific purpose which can be found in Jeremiah:

> *To root out and to pull down, to destroy and to throw down, to build and to plant.*
>
> *Jeremiah 1:10*

CHAPTER 2

UNDERSTANDING GOD'S LANGUAGE FOR US

It's important to understand the language of God and how He communicates with us. The most helpful way of understanding His language is to read in the Bible how Jesus communicated with His disciples and with the people He ministered to. It's clear that He spoke in parables. This was to fulfill the prophecy given to Isaiah.

And He said, "Go and tell this people: 'Keep on hearing, but do not understand; Keep on seeing, but do not perceive.' Make the heart of this people dull, and their ears heavy, and shut their eyes; lest they see with their eyes, and hear with their ears, and understand with their heart, and return and be healed."

Isaiah 6:9-10

The account was repeated in Matthew.

And the disciples came and said to Him, "Why do You speak to them in parables?" He answered and said to them, "Because it has been given to you to know the mysteries of the kingdom of heaven, but to them it has not been given. For whoever has, to him more will be given, and he will have abundance; but whoever does not have, even what he has will be taken away from him. Therefore I speak to them in parables, because seeing they do not see, and hearing they do not hear, nor do they understand. And in them the prophecy of Isaiah is fulfilled, which says: 'Hearing you will hear and shall not understand, and seeing you will see and not perceive; for the hearts of this people have grown dull. Their ears are hard of hearing, and their eyes they have closed, lest they should see with their eyes and hear with their ears, lest they should understand with their hearts and turn, so that I should heal them.'"

Matthew 13:10-15

All these things Jesus spoke to the multitude in parables; and without a parable He did not speak to them, that it might be fulfilled which was spoken by the prophet, saying: "I will open My mouth in parables; I will utter things kept secret from the foundation of the world."

Matthew 13:34-35

The same account is found in the book of Mark:

But when He was alone, those around Him with the twelve asked Him about the parable. And He said to them, "To you it has been given to know the mystery of the kingdom of God; but to those who are outside, all things come in parables, so that 'Seeing they may see and not perceive, and hearing they may hear and not understand; lest they should turn, and their sins be forgiven them.'"

Mark 4:10-12

How often have you awakened from a dream or seen a vision and been stumped by its meaning? According to Isaiah, this was God's plan all along. God wants us to pursue the understanding and interpretation of His plans and direction for our lives. He wants to make sure that our hearts have not grown dull and that we truly want to seek His face with all our heart. Dreams and visions are meant to be a mystery, but we must seek His face and His Word to gain the understanding and interpretation of them.

The Bible says that God speaks to us in parables; therefore, this is His language for us.

> *And the word of the LORD came to me, saying, "Son of man, pose a riddle, and speak a parable to the house of Israel, and say, 'Thus says the Lord GOD...'"*
>
> *Ezekiel 17:1-3*

> *Then I said, "Ah, Lord GOD! They say of me, 'Does he not speak parables?'"*
>
> *Ezekiel 20:49*

> *And utter a parable to the rebellious house, and say to them, "Thus says the Lord God..."*
>
> *Ezekiel 24:3*

> *Give ear, O my people, to my law; incline your ears to the words of my mouth. I will open my mouth in a parable; I will utter dark sayings of old, which we have heard and known, and our fathers have told us. We will not hide them from their children, telling to the generation to come the praises of the LORD, and His strength and His wonderful works that He has done.*
>
> *Psalm 78:1-4*

A parable is a simple story which is told to convey a moral truth. In these parables, we must look for the underlying message and then seek His Word concerning that message.

He speaks to us a mystery or a riddle (a parable), and we must seek Him to gain understanding of what He is trying to say to us. Our dreams are basically parables or allegories of His plans and purposes for our lives.

It says in the Word that Jesus is the same yesterday, today, and forever (Hebrews 13:8); therefore, we must understand that His way of communicating with us today remains the same as it was since the fall of man.

The reason the world has such a hard time interpreting dreams is because they don't have the Holy Spirit to give them understanding, and they don't understand the way God speaks through His parables.

> *But when He was alone, those around Him with the twelve asked Him about the parable. And He said to them, "To you it has been given to know the mystery of the kingdom of God; but to those who are outside, all things come in parables, so that 'Seeing they may see and not perceive, and hearing they may hear and not understand; lest they should turn, and their sins be forgiven them.'" And He said to them, "Do you not understand this parable? How then will you understand all the parables? The sower sows the word. And these are the ones by the wayside where the word is sown. When they hear, Satan comes immediately and takes away the word that was sown in their hearts. These likewise are the ones on stony ground who, when they hear the word, immediately receive it with gladness; and they have no root in themselves, and so endure only for a time. Afterward, when tribulation or persecution arises for the word's sake, immediately they stumble. Now these are the ones sown among thorns; they are the ones who hear the word, and the cares of this world, the deceitfulness of riches, and the desires for other things entering in choke the word, and it becomes unfruitful. But these are the ones sown on good ground, those who hear the word, accept it, and bear fruit: some thirtyfold, some sixty, and some a hundred."*
>
> *Mark 4:10-20*

It is clear that God gives people dreams, and some even visions, but these dreams and visions will remain a mystery until they want to seek His face or until someone who has been given understanding by the Holy Spirit interprets their dreams or visions.

The Lord speaks differently to each one of us because we were all created uniquely, but we must begin to understand His language for us as individuals. We've all had different experiences in life, and that will affect how He speaks to us. How we grew up, the influences around us, and the culture we live in will affect how we see different things. Objects and people may mean something to one person, but another thing to someone else. We must understand who the dreamer is and what these objects mean to the dreamer before we assume an interpretation. Different cultures have different life experiences and points of view. This is why it's so important to be full of the Holy Spirit when we interpret dreams. God knows the dreams and the dreamers, and His language for each one of us is individual and specific. It would be foolish to rely on our own earthly knowledge and understanding when interpreting our dreams.

One of the best examples I've found to explain this would be the dog. Many people love dogs, but there are just as many people who are afraid of dogs. The Bible doesn't say very many good things about dogs, but to many of us they are our best friends. We must understand what a dog means to the dreamer and the role of the dog in the dream before we assume its interpretation.

I have a dog named Gracie. I dream about her often, and her role in my dream is always the same. She represents grace and God's grace for me. Whenever I see her in my dream, I know that it has to do with God's grace for me or His grace in the given situation. At least I know that His grace is involved, and I can trust that God is with me and walking me through the trials and tribulations of life. It's interesting that my dog does not represent the same dogs we read about in the Word of God. God knows that my dog, Gracie, is dear to my heart and that I would understand His grace represented through her.

One must realize that not all objects can be found in the Bible. One example would be the guerilla. There were no guerillas found in Israel or in the regions and territories where the Bible was written. We cannot discount the fact that people do have dreams about guerillas. Therefore, we must look at the characteristics of the animal and what they mean to us. Another example would be the many forms of transportation found in the world today, such as bikes, cars, trucks, buses, trains, airplanes, etc. I can't tell you how many times I've dreamt about the various vehicles in the world. So, because they are not in the Bible, does this mean we discount their significance in the dream? No, they are significant in most dreams and must be looked at closely. To interpret these vehicles, we must look at their function and purpose of operation. Many details can influence their meaning but it is important to know whom they serve and how they are operated or used.

Very often we may have a dream that we cannot understand or interpret, and it may leave us bewildered by its message. This doesn't mean that we throw it away. It is important to journal our dreams so that when the right time comes for the mystery to be revealed, the dream is there to bring confirmation to our life experiences. These are very often prophetic dreams for the future. Joseph of Egypt had such a dream:

> *Now Joseph had a dream, and he told it to his brothers; and they hated him even more. So he said to them, "Please hear this dream which I have dreamed: There we were, binding sheaves in the field. Then behold, my sheaf arose and also stood upright; and indeed your sheaves stood all around and bowed down to my sheaf." And his brothers said to him, "Shall you indeed reign over us? Or shall you indeed have dominion over us?" So they hated him even more for his dreams and for his words. Then he dreamed still another dream and told it to his brothers, and said, "Look, I have dreamed another dream. And this time, the sun, the moon, and the eleven stars bowed down to me." So he told it to his father and his brothers; and his father rebuked him and said to him, "What is this dream that you have dreamed? Shall your mother and I and your brothers indeed come to bow down to the earth before you?" And his brothers envied him, but his father kept the matter in mind.*
>
> *Genesis 37:5-11*

It is important that we ponder and wait upon every mystery and word from the Lord, for if it is truly from the Lord it may tarry, but it will come to pass. God gives us dreams which are sometimes concealed for an appointed time. If it's truly from Him, though it is concealed and though it waits (tarries), it will surely come to pass, in His timing, not ours. Sometimes He is testing our faithfulness to His Word. Are we willing to wait for His timing, or do we push to cause our own effects or interpretation or even give up on waiting? Take these dreams to Him in prayer.

> *For the vision is yet for an appointed time; but at the end it will speak, and it will not lie. Though it tarries wait for it; because it will surely come.*
>
> *Habakkuk 2:3*

THE PURPOSE OF DREAMS AND VISIONS:

The purpose of dreams and visions is to bring about change in our life and to cause us to live in His will and in His plan. Dreams and vision are no good to us unless we make them real and unless we claim them as they come. If your desire is to obey the Holy Spirit, then you must walk out what has been revealed to you in your dreams and visions. He desires that we not go astray from His plan and His way. He desires that we strive to be holy and walk in His paths of righteousness.

> *He who keeps instruction is in the way of life, but he who refuses correction goes astray.*
>
> *Proverbs 10:17*

The Bible says:

> *For the vision is yet for an appointed time; But at the end it will speak, and it will not lie. Though it tarries, wait for it; because it will surely come, it will not tarry.*
>
> *Habakkuk 2:3*

Many people lack the power to wait for God's appointed times in their lives and they lose the vision. They forget about it or they put it on the shelf or they neglect their passion for change. Many even lose faith that it will even come to pass. We have a responsibility to keep the vision alive, to keep the fire burning until we have actually walked through the vision and seen it come to pass. The Bible says that the vision may tarry, but we must wait for it, we must wait for those appointed times because they will surely come and they will not lie.

So what do we do when the Lord gives us a dream or vision? First and foremost, we must examine the dream or vision and seek its interpretation. When the interpretation has been found, we are to walk it out and apply it to our own personal lives. Take every dream personally before you conclude it to be about someone else. Generally speaking, it would be safe to say that ninety-five percent of our dreams are usually for the dreamer rather than for other people. Some dreams may be hard to receive, but remember God desires that we walk in righteousness, and He wants to bring correction to us so that we won't go astray.

> *I will bless the Lord who has given me counsel; my heart also instructs me in the night seasons. I have set the Lord always before me; because He is at my right hand I shall not be moved.*
>
> *Psalm 16:7-8*

> *My son, do not despise the chastening of the Lord, nor detest His correction; for whom the Lord loves He corrects, just as a father the son in whom he delights.*
>
> *Proverbs 3:11-12*

There are many reasons why the Lord may speak to us in a dream or vision; I call these reasons "dream purposes."

DREAM PURPOSES:

- **Directional**: to lead and guide us through our life situations
- **Correctional**: to show us the error of our ways

- **Encouragement**: to help us so that we won't fall into discouragement
- **Warning**: to warn us of potential problems or issues
- **Intercession**: to cause us to pray
- **Words of knowledge and wisdom**: to enlighten us of unknown situations and to bring solutions to the problems
- **Prophetic**: to speak destiny into our lives or the lives of others
- **Revelation**: to give spiritual insight or even creativity for inventions

God does not speak without purpose; therefore, dreams and visions from God come to us with a purpose. His purposes always require action. Once we have found the purpose, we can walk in the light of knowledge and understanding of His truth for our life. He is the light which illuminates the darkness, and His word comes to us for one reason:

To root out and to pull down, to destroy and to throw down, to build and to plant.

Jeremiah 1:10

CHAPTER 3

INTERPRETING YOUR DREAMS AND VISIONS

So how do you interpret your dreams and visions? This is a method I refer to as the "Process of Interpretation." This process should be followed after receiving any dream or vision from the Lord.

PROCESS OF INTERPRETATION:

1. Write down the dream or vision.

Write down your dream or vision immediately, before it's forgotten. I can't tell you how many times I've awakened with a dream from the Lord, but held off writing it down until after breakfast or even later in the day. Needless to say, many of those dreams were lost and details forgotten. Don't take the chance of losing His voice and direction for your life. Another excellent tool I've found helpful is a digital tape recorder set by my bedside. If I have a dream in the middle of the night and I'm too tired to take the time to write it down, I simply whisper it into the recorder and write it down the next morning. After it is written down, develop a title for the dream. The best way to do this is to decide what the primary focus of the dream is. What stands out to you most? Usually your first impression is the best one. Don't make this a scientific process; just keep it simple.

2. Pray for the Lord to reveal the interpretation to you.

You must take this dream to prayer asking God for understanding and relying on the Holy Spirit for the dream's interpretation. *This is the most important aspect of dream interpretation.*

3. Circle the words of importance and focus.

Circle the words of focus and the words that appear to be most important, and then find out what the Word of God says about these words. Very often, the definitions of these words will lead you directly to a passage of Scripture that will bring understanding to the dream or vision. To find the focus, ask yourself these questions: Who is this dream about? Is it about the dreamer or someone else? Is it about a people group, a city, a nation, or someone else? If you have discovered the right focus, the details will support that focus.

It's best to first get a broader picture of the dream and then examine it word by word. Writing down the main facts will help you find the focus of the dream or vision. While details are important, be aware that sometimes those details can get in the way of a bigger, more important message. Once the theme is discovered, the details may be examined.

In the first year of Belshazzar king of Babylon, Daniel had a dream and visions of his head while on his bed. Then he wrote down the dream, telling the main facts.

Daniel 7:1

4. Look at the dream or vision in the form of a parable and reduce it to its simplest form. Ask yourself, "What is the underlying theme or message?"

It is important that we look at the dream or vision as a parable. Since we know that a parable is a simple story told to convey a moral truth, we must look for the underlying message and then ask these questions:

- What is the focus of the dream?
- What is your role in the dream? What are the roles of the other people in the dream?
- What is being said, and what are people doing?
- What is the underlying theme or message?
- Can that theme be found in the Word of God, and what does it say about it?

5. Using the given words and their definitions, fill in any pertinent details.

Even though I urge you to focus on the facts of the dream and the larger picture, sometimes the details can be significant. Don't get lost on a rabbit trail, but make sure you don't miss any of what the Lord wants you to know or understand. Remember, God is in the details and His Word is exhaustive. Get everything He has for you.

6. Back it up with Scripture.

All dreams need to be tested by the Word of God. God will not contradict His Word. His Scripture will be in agreement with what He is telling you. If you can't find Scripture to back it up, the dream or vision probably is not from God.

7. Determine your response to the message in the dream or vision.

When God speaks, have listening and hearing ears. Receive His Word with gladness and obedience. God is constantly molding and shaping us into His image. Be that willing vessel. Your response will determine the outcome of God's Word for your life and even the life of others.

We must understand our physical, emotional, and spiritual state when interpreting our dreams. It will soon become evident if the dream is not from God. The Word of God will not back it up. If the

41

demonic realm or the soul has provoked these dreams, they will reveal the works of the enemy or the dealings of iniquity in your life. Dreams can also be caused by physical illness or induced by drugs or alcohol.

To help you get started, I've included a couple of example dreams. If you follow the process of interpretation of these dreams, and apply that process and the Word of God to the interpretation of your own dreams, I'm confident that you will be on the road to better understanding what God is saying to you in your dreams and visions.

EXAMPLE DREAM 1:

This example dream was a warning dream for both my husband and me for the purpose of intercession and to prepare us for the coming events. It is possible, however, to change coming events through our own intercession.

DREAM: Train Tracks Dream and Vision

I dreamed that Steve and I were riding a <u>two-person</u> bike down a dirt road. Steve was in front and I was in back. Suddenly, we came to a set of <u>train tracks</u>. The track itself was not like a regular track. It had a concave upper edge, so that we could fit the tires of our bike in the groove of the track. This allowed us to <u>ride directly on the track without falling to the right or to the left</u>. About five hundred yards down the track, we came to a <u>bridge</u> and proceeded to cross the bridge. Down below was a <u>muddy, turbulent river,</u> so rapid that the force of the waves seemed to crawl up the pylons of the bridge. Steve was riding in front, so <u>I wasn't able to look</u> far enough ahead of me to see that the train tracks were <u>sabotaged and blown up</u> in the middle of the bridge. Steve apparently <u>wasn't watching</u> either so we both fell into the muddy river. I woke up.

I fell asleep again and dreamed the exact same dream, only this time <u>we stopped the bike before we fell in</u>. I woke up.

This time, while I was awake, I had a vision of the same scenario, only this time the tracks went all the way across and we made it safely to the other side.

WORD DEFINITIONS:

Two-person bike:	Tandem, one behind another working together for a common purpose, partnership, team, agreement, union.
Train tracks:	Path, discipleship path, way of holiness, route, trail, a course laid out, awareness of a fact or progression.
Bridge:	Transition, difficult change in life, to pass over (troubled or easy circumstances), to overcome obstacles, leaving the old and coming into the new, a means of crossing over an obstacle, passageway, to cross over to the other side.
Muddy:	Not clear, deception, caused by the flesh, confusion, to make unclear, blurred or obscure, cloudy.
Turbulent:	Causing disturbance through violence, agitation, or tumult; rage; the voice of the enemy; tempest; the judgment of the Lord.
River:	The Holy Spirit; Jesus, the King; Spirit of life (living waters); flowing in the Spirit; to flow in the channels of God; bathing or cleansing; baptism (by water and by the Spirit); healing; irrigation and provision; peace; blessing of God; God's delights; peace; life; refreshing; revival; tears; to be overwhelmed or overcome.
Bomb (blown up):	To attack, sabotage, impact, explosive, snare, to undermine the progress of, forcibly moved, shatter, destroy, deliberate destruction, hindrance by the enemy, wreck, danger.

Wasn't looking or wasn't watching:	Unaware, not looking ahead, ignorant, lacking knowledge, unknowing, oblivious.
Stopped:	Halt, to bring one's activity to an end, final point of a journey (IDIOM: to stop in your tracks).

SHORT INTERPRETATION:

This is a warning dream.

Although you are working together with a common purpose, be watchful of what is ahead so that you don't fall prey to your own flesh and to the snares of wicked men who seek to destroy you. Keep your eyes fixed on Him and He will bring you to a safe harbor.

Psalm 124:2-8, 2 Timothy 4:5, Isaiah 35:8-10.

LONG INTERPRETATION:

(This was a warning dream for Steve and me for the purpose of intercession, for an event that would occur more than two years later.)

It shows that Steve and I were operating in unity and working together for a common purpose in both our marriage and in our ministry (two-person bike). Steve was the head and I was backing him up. We were staying on track and not falling to the left or the right (train tracks).

The bridge represented a means by which we were to cross over a coming obstacle and a time of transition, a way of crossing over to the other side. The muddy turbulent water represented a great deception of the flesh and how our own flesh could possibly cloud our vision and cause us to fall into the great deception.

The fact that Steve wasn't looking and I wasn't watching shows how we were both unaware of the coming great deception. The blown-up tracks represented the coming sabotage and potential hindrance to our ministry. The fact that we weren't watching caused us to fall prey to the confusion and flesh of man (muddy turbulent river).

The second dream shows that we were now aware of the coming destruction and deception, and we were able to stop in our tracks before falling prey to the flesh.

Jesus wants us to go into life's situations with eyes wide open. This is the purpose of the third vision. When we operate in His Spirit and not in our flesh, He makes a way and causes us to overcome and walk in His paths of righteousness. If we seek Him with all our heart and follow His instructions, He will bring us to a safe harbor (we made it safely to the other side).

SCRIPTURE REFERENCE:

If it had not been the Lord who was on our side, when men rose up against us, then they would have swallowed us alive, when their wrath was kindled against us; then the waters would have overwhelmed us, the stream would have gone over our soul; then the swollen waters would have gone over our soul. Blessed be the Lord, who has not given us as prey to their teeth. Our soul has escaped as a bird from the snare of the fowlers; the snare is broken, and we have escaped. Our help is in the name of the Lord, who made heaven and earth.

Psalm 124:2-8

But you be watchful in all things, endure afflictions, do the work of an evangelist, fulfill your ministry.

2 Timothy 4:5

A highway shall be there, and a road, and it shall be called the Highway of Holiness. The unclean shall not pass over it, but it shall be for others. Whoever walks the road, although a fool, shall not go astray. No lion shall be there, nor shall any ravenous beast go up on it; it shall not be found there. But the redeemed shall walk there, and the ransomed of the Lord shall return, and come to Zion with singing, with ever-

lasting joy on their heads. They shall obtain joy and glad-ness, and sorrow and sighing shall flee away.

Isaiah 35:8-10

This dream remained a mystery to both my husband and me for nearly two years after it was given. But I knew it was important and that the mystery would very soon be revealed. I recorded the dream in my journal and took it to prayer until we finally experienced the real-life situation. Because of the dream, the Lord had prepared our hearts and reminded us to keep our eyes fixed on Him during the trial and tribulation, and, because of it, He brought us to safe harbor.

Many people like to stop with just a short interpretation, especially when interpreting the dreams of others, but I find it helpful to take it a step further when interpreting my own dreams. I'm a visual person and so expanding it with a longer interpretation helps me get a bigger and fuller picture of what the Lord is saying to me. We must, however, be careful not to get hung up on every single word and possibly get caught up on a rabbit trail and off the beaten path. Keep the main thing, the main thing. The focus needs to remain the focus.

EXAMPLE DREAM 2:

This second dream was a prophetic dream given to a friend of mine for the purpose of intercession and to speak destiny into her life and ministry. Please keep in mind that this dream has been unedited and is recorded as it was first expressed. Most dreams sound a little incoherent when they first come out, but it's important to listen and study the first words chosen. Sometimes, if you rephrase dreams, the interpreter may lose those whole first impressions of the dream.

DREAM: Musketeers and Weapons

I dreamed that <u>seven men</u>, I included, were <u>dressed in the appearance of Musketeers</u>. Each of us had an <u>individually unique modern weapon</u>. We were all in a rectangular-shaped room, <u>no windows, and one door</u>. We were <u>waiting for our enemies</u> to come. While we were practicing with our weapons I noticed that <u>each weapon was fashioned for one enemy</u>. I knew that it would not work on anything else. Suddenly, I knew that the <u>enemy I was targeting was standing outside the door</u>. I <u>opened the door</u> and he stood facing me. He was <u>armored from neck to feet</u> with large shoulder pads of metal. Nothing was penetrable except for his <u>head; it was uncovered</u>. He was extremely <u>handsome and had long blond hair and blue eyes</u>. It was <u>raining outside, straight down in sheets, and it was very dark</u>. About <u>forty feet</u> away was another building, same shape and size as the one we were in with no windows. To my right at the corner of that building was a <u>light below the roofline</u>. <u>Because of the light I was able to see that about twenty feet from the ends of the building</u>, further to my right, was a <u>power pole</u>. As soon as I opened the door I fired my weapon (it looked like a fat rounded steel water gun with two handles), and <u>it shot out a liquid that looked like water</u>. As soon as the liquid hit my enemy he screamed violently and <u>ran like an ape toward the power pole</u>. I kept firing and hitting him (it appeared to be burning him) until <u>he took a forty-foot leap to the top of the power pole</u>. He <u>sneered and laughed</u> at me then jumped down and disappeared behind the other building. I <u>looked to the left into the utter darkness with expectancy for him to appear</u> and awoke.

WORD DEFINITIONS:

Seven: Perfection, completeness, revelation, rest, finished, perfect consecration, holy convocation, fulfillment.

Musketeers: Soldiers, warriors, bodyguard, all for one and one for all, unity of the brethren, Christians, bodyguard, vessels of honor, loyalty.

Modern: Current or present times, advanced style or technique.

Weapon:
: Offensive or defensive tool, armor, spiritual tools for combat, tools of warfare, used in attack, used to overcome one's adversary, to arm and ready oneself with protection, indignation.

Enemy:
: Adversary, those who oppose, satan, the gospel's enemy, a rival, opponent, oppressor, one who sows evil, the accuser of the brethren, deceiver, wickedness, Christians are commanded to love them, death.

Neck:
: Yoke, bondage, servitude, triumph over a foe, rebel or resist (to stiffen or harden one's neck), stubborn, self-willed.

Feet:
: Walk, way, path, course of walking, manner of living, conduct, behavior, discipleship (as in "to sit at the feet of"), teachable, subjection, submission, stability, preparation, humility and worship (as in "to fall at the feet of"), dance, conquest (as in "to put under the feet"), hospitality (as in "to wash the feet of"), great love (as in "to kiss the feet of"), rejection (as in "shake off the dust of your feet"), preaching the gospel.

Head (uncovered):
: No cover or protection, no spiritual covering, no insurance or security, bare, naked, unclean, exposed, revealed.

Handsome:
: Pleasing to the eye, beautiful, angel of light (the devil), the deceiver.

Rain:
: Teaching, wisdom, revival, restoration, refreshing, life, Word of God, depression, trial, disappointment (to "rain on someone's parade"), heavenly provision and blessing, God's judgment and wrath.

Dark:
: Containing no light, outside the presence of God, unfruitful works, affliction, moral depravity, ignorance and unbelief, chaos, evil, death, hell, everlasting punishment of the wicked.

Forty: Generation; period of temptation, struggle, and testing; time of spiritual training through trials and difficulty; testing; judgment.

Light: God, His truth, the Word of God, the glory of God, revealed, exposed, to guide one's way, to reflect, the eyes of man, to illuminate the darkness.

Twenty: To judge, tried, to govern, to oversee, head of the house, fit or unfit for service, able to go to war.

Water: Word of the Lord, Jesus Christ, spiritual growth, teaching, knowledge, refreshing, peace, eternal life, to quench one's thirst, regeneration, cleansing, purification, baptism, sanctification, salvation, life-giving, irrigating.

Burning: Cleansing, to purge, cleansing, the presence of God (the burning bush), intense heat, passionate, test or trial, jealousy, punishment, God's wrath and anger, to consume with fire.

Power pole: Power source, to raise or hold up the source of power, high position of authority over others, one who has control or authority, to supply with power, ability to function, plugged in, ability to affect, physical might, energy to do work, strength, brawn, muscle.

Ape: The uncivilized world, rough, intimidation, boaster, proud, clumsy, crude person, harsh, inferior quality, lack of civilized character, uncultivated, barbaric, brutish, wild, ill-bred, unrefined, unpolished, primitive, foolish, mischief, deceitful, not honest (as in "monkey business"), wickedness.

Sneered and laughed: Scoffer (Ps. 73:8), mockery.

Left: Spiritual weakness of man, rejection, feebleness, handicap, disadvantaged position, not skillful, to walk away from one's calling or purpose, ill warning of future events, unlucky, north.

SHORT INTERPRETATION:

This dream is a prophetic dream for the purpose of intercession and to speak destiny into your life and ministry.

You (my friend) are a warrior with a strong loyalty to your King and are being fashioned for a specific purpose of warfare (*individually unique modern weapon*) for the kingdom of God. Your weapon is clearly the truths and revelation of the Word of God (*water*). Your enemy is one of deception and without spiritual covering. He is a scoffer and mocker of the true Word of God. This enemy can be found at the door of the church and also out in the world. Your weapon of truth will cause his true colors to come forth. Stay under the authority placed over you and you will be able to see and know your enemy when he comes. Speak the truth in love and be ready in season and out of season.

> *Psalm 119:73-80; 1 John 1:5-7; 1 John 3:10-1; 2 Corinthians 10:3-6, 11:13-15; 2 Timothy 3:13; Matthew 5:43-45; 1 Corinthians 16:9; Romans 12:20-21; Isaiah 55:10-11; Hebrews 12:29; Deuteronomy 9:3; Isaiah 44:25; 1 Peter 5:8-9; 2 Timothy 3:1-7; Psalm 73:6-11; Ephesians 6:10-20; 2 Timothy 4:1-5; Philippians 1:27-30; Job 24:13-25.*

LONG INTERPRETATION:

This dream is a prophetic dream for the purpose of intercession and to speak destiny into your life and ministry.

The seven men represent your role with the body of Christ and the complete unity of the brethren operating in one accord. They are warriors with an "All for one and One for all" loyalty (*Musketeers*). You are a warrior with a strong loyalty to your King and are being fashioned for a specific purpose of warfare (*individually unique modern weapon*) for the kingdom of God.

> *Your hands have made me and fashioned me; give me understanding, that I may learn Your commandments. Those who*

fear You will be glad when they see me, because I have hoped in Your word. I know, O LORD, that Your judgments are right, and that in faithfulness You have afflicted me. Let, I pray, Your merciful kindness be for my comfort, according to Your word to Your servant. Let Your tender mercies come to me, that I may live; for Your law is my delight. Let the proud be ashamed, for they treated me wrongfully with false-hood; but I will meditate on Your precepts. Let those who fear You turn to me, those who know Your testimonies. Let my heart be blameless regarding Your statutes, that I may not be ashamed.

Psalm 119:73-80

The rectangular room with no windows and one door represents that single purpose and single destiny for your life and ministry. Practice is the preparation of becoming proficient in your faith and in the truth of God's Word. We need to practice truth (1 John 1:5-10), righteousness, and love (1 John 3:10-11) (*practicing with our weapons*) in all godliness.

This is the message which we have heard from Him and declare to you, that God is light and in Him is no darkness at all. If we say that we have fellowship with Him, and walk in darkness, we lie and do not <u>practice the truth</u>. But if we walk in the light as He is in the light, we have fellowship with one another, and the blood of Jesus Christ His Son cleanses us from all sin.

1 John 1:5-7

In this the children of God and the children of the devil are manifest: Whoever does not practice righteousness is not of God, nor is he who does not love his brother. For this is the message that you heard from the beginning, that we should love one another.

1 John 3:10-11

It says in the Bible that satan will come as an angel of light. This would explain the fact that he appears to be handsome with blond hair and blue eyes. Your adversary appears to have the face of deception. The fact that his head is uncovered shows that your enemy is probably one who has no spiritual covering and is exposed for satan to have open access to his mind. This enemy could be found in the world or even in the church.

For such are false apostles, deceitful workers, transforming themselves into apostles of Christ. And no wonder! For Satan himself transforms himself into an angel of light. Therefore it is no great thing if his ministers also transform themselves into ministers of righteousness, whose end will be according to their works.

2 Corinthians 11:13-15

But evil men and impostors will grow worse and worse, deceiving and being deceived.

2 Timothy 3:13

The Lord has made it clear in His Word that He will rain on both the righteous and the wicked.

You have heard that it was said, "You shall love your neighbor and hate your enemy." But I say to you, love your enemies, bless those who curse you, do good to those who hate you, and pray for those who spitefully use you and persecute you, that you may be sons of your Father in heaven; for He makes His sun rise on the evil and on the good, and sends rain on the just and on the unjust.

Matthew 5:43-45

The darkness represents the spiritual atmosphere of the situation. Since God is light, then darkness represents being outside of the presence of God (1 John 1:5-7).

The forty feet between buildings represents a period of spiritual training through the tests and trials of your life and ministry.

You are apparently in a period of training for war. The light below the roofline represents our role as Christians in a dark world. We need to shine our light before men and stay under the covering set over us. This submission to authority will allow us to see our adversary clearly and provide us with the spiritual covering necessary to operate in the Lord's supernatural power without being taken out by satan's tactics and schemes. When our lamp is lit, we are able to see the enemy before us and go to war (*Because of the light, I was able to see about twenty feet from the ends of the building*).

You opened the door of your destiny and purpose and fired your weapon.

For a great and effective door has opened to me, and there are many adversaries.

1 Corinthians 16:9

Your enemy is a specific one, just as your weapon will be specific for that enemy. Your weapon is the truth and revelation of the Word of God. The gun represents your mouth, but also the mouth of God, and out of His mouth comes the Word of God and His living water.

Therefore "If your enemy is hungry, feed him; if he is thirsty, give him a drink; for in so doing you will heap coals of fire on his head. Do not be overcome by evil, but overcome evil with good."

Romans 12:20-21

For though we walk in the flesh, we do not war according to the flesh. For the weapons of our warfare are not carnal but mighty in God for pulling down strongholds, casting down arguments and every high thing that exalts itself against the knowledge of God, bringing every thought into captivity to the obedience of Christ, and being ready to punish all disobedience when your obedience is fulfilled.

2 Corinthians 10:3-6

The truth of the Word burned your enemy because that is the purpose of God's refining fire. God is a consuming fire and His fire will burn up all that is not of Him. This fire will bring light to the world. His Word goes forth and does not return to Him void.

For as the rain comes down, and the snow from heaven, and do not return there, but water the earth, and make it bring forth and bud, that it may give seed to the sower and bread to the eater, so shall My word be that goes forth from My mouth; it shall not return to Me void, but it shall accomplish what I please, and it shall prosper in the thing for which I sent it.

Isaiah 55:10-11

For our God is a consuming fire.

Hebrews 12:29

Therefore understand today that the LORD your God is He who goes over before you as a consuming fire. He will destroy them and bring them down before you; so you shall drive them out and destroy them quickly, as the LORD has said to you.

Deuteronomy 9:3

The ape represents the true character and motive of your adversary. You began to see his true colors once you had spoken the truth of God's Word. This enemy is a brutal babbler and a scoffer, one who lacks civilized character, is proud, foolish, and deceitful.

Who frustrates the signs of the babblers, and drives diviners mad; who turns wise men backward, and makes their knowledge foolishness...

Isaiah 44:25

Be sober, be vigilant; because your adversary the devil walks about like a roaring lion, seeking whom he may devour. Resist him, steadfast in the faith, knowing that the same sufferings are experienced by your brotherhood in the world.

1 Peter 5:8-9

But know this, that in the last days perilous times will come: For men will be lovers of themselves, lovers of money, boasters, proud, blasphemers, disobedient to parents, unthankful, unholy, unloving, unforgiving, slanderers, without self-control, brutal, despisers of good, traitors, headstrong, haughty, lovers of pleasure rather than lovers of God, having a form of godliness but denying its power. And from such people turn away! For of this sort are those who creep into households and make captives of gullible women loaded down with sins, led away by various lusts, always learning and never able to come to the knowledge of the truth.

2 Timothy 3:1-7

Therefore pride serves as their necklace; violence covers them like a garment. Their eyes bulge with abundance; they have more than heart could wish. They scoff and speak wickedly concerning oppression; they speak loftily. They set their mouth against the heavens, and their tongue walks through the earth. Therefore his people return here, and waters of a full cup are drained by them. And they say, "How does God know? And is there knowledge in the Most High?"

Psalm 73:6-11

The power pole represents a manmade power source and the high position of authority and control that this enemy has over others. It represents the enemy's reliance on his own power and physical might, rather than on the power of God. This enemy will exalt himself loftily over his foes through pride and arrogance.

When you looked to the left with expectancy for him to appear, it represents your understanding of your adversary. He is wicked and you must be prepared at all times, having been girded with the full armor of the Lord that you may be able to stand against the wiles of the devil.

> *Finally, my brethren, be strong in the Lord and in the power of His might. Put on the whole armor of God, that you may be able to stand against the wiles of the devil. For we do not wrestle against flesh and blood, but against principalities, against powers, against the rulers of the darkness of this age, against spiritual hosts of wickedness in the heavenly places. Therefore take up the whole armor of God, that you may be able to withstand in the evil day, and having done all, to stand. Stand therefore, having girded your waist with truth, having put on the breastplate of righteousness, and having shod your feet with the preparation of the gospel of peace; above all, taking the shield of faith with which you will be able to quench all the fiery darts of the wicked one. And take the helmet of salvation, and the sword of the Spirit, which is the word of God; praying always with all prayer and supplication in the Spirit, being watchful to this end with all perseverance and supplication for all the saints— and for me, that utterance may be given to me, that I may open my mouth boldly to make known the mystery of the gospel, for which I am an ambassador in chains; that in it I may speak boldly, as I ought to speak.*
>
> *Ephesians 6:10-20*

The Lord has a specific plan and purpose for your life, and He has fashioned you for battle and girded you with truth and the Word of God. Your weapon of truth will cause your enemy's true colors to come forth. Stay under the authority placed over you and you will be able to see and know your enemy when he comes. Speak the truth in love. Be watching and waiting for your enemy and ready for war in season and out of season.

> *I charge you therefore before God and the Lord Jesus Christ, who will judge the living and the dead at His appearing and His kingdom: Preach the word! Be ready in season and out*

of season. Convince, rebuke, exhort, with all longsuffering and teaching. For the time will come when they will not endure sound doctrine, but according to their own desires, because they have itching ears, they will heap up for themselves teachers; and they will turn their ears away from the truth, and be turned aside to fables. But you be watchful in all things, endure afflictions, do the work of an evangelist, fulfill your ministry.

2 Timothy 4:1-5

SCRIPTURE REFERENCE:

Only let your conduct be worthy of the gospel of Christ, so that whether I come and see you or am absent, I may hear of your affairs, that you stand fast in one spirit, with one mind striving together for the faith of the gospel, and not in any way terrified by your adversaries, which is to them a proof of perdition, but to you of salvation, and that from God. For to you it has been granted on behalf of Christ, not only to believe in Him, but also to suffer for His sake, having the same conflict which you saw in me and now hear is in me.

Philippians 1:27-30

There are those who rebel against the light; they do not know its ways nor abide in its paths. The murderer rises with the light; he kills the poor and needy; and in the night he is like a thief. The eye of the adulterer waits for the twilight, saying, "No eye will see me"; and he disguises his face. In the dark they break into houses which they marked for themselves in the daytime; they do not know the light. For the morning is the same to them as the shadow of death; if someone recognizes them, they are in the terrors of the shadow of death. They should be swift on the face of the waters, their portion should be cursed in the earth, so that no one would turn into the way of their vineyards. As drought and heat consume the snow waters, so the grave consumes those who have sinned. The womb should forget him, the worm should feed sweetly on him; he should be remembered no more, and wickedness should be broken like a tree. For he preys on the barren who do not bear, and does no good for the widow. But God draws the mighty away with His power; He rises up, but no man is sure of life. He gives them security, and they rely on it; yet His eyes are on their ways. They are exalted for a little while, then they are gone. They are brought low; they are taken out of the way like all others; they dry out like the heads of grain. Now if it is not so, who will prove me a liar, and make my speech worth nothing?

Job 24:13-25

So now you're ready to get started. I hope this resource has revealed to you the language of the Lord for your life and has taught you to seek His Word for the answers to your dreams and visions. Although it is not an exhaustive reference guide, I pray that you have learned to search out the Word of God for your interpretation needs. His Word is truly exhaustive and lacking in nothing. God is faithful if we seek Him with all our heart.

A

Abortion – *Rejected:* To cast out whatever is impure or undesirable; termination; termination of ministry; to refuse; to withhold love from; to throw out; to disapprove; to bring or come to an end; to cancel; to let go; rejection of the innocent.

Reference:Ex 21:22-24; Job 3:16; 10:19; Jer 20:17; Lam 4:10-11; Hos 9:14-16; 1 Thes 4:8.

Adoption – *Sonship:* Inheritance; redemption; accepted into Sonship; access to the Father; to receive into one's family; believer's relationship to God.

Reference:Ex 2:10; Est 2:7; Rom 4:16; 8:14-16, 23; 9:3-5; Gal 3:26-27; 4:4-6.

Adultery – *Unfaithfulness:* Fornication; works of the flesh; nakedness; nakedness uncovered; harlotry; idolatry; lust; uncleanness.

Reference:Ex 20:14; Pr 2:16-22; Ezek 16:36-38; Mt 5:27-28; Gal 5:19-21.

Airplane – *Person or ministry:* Church; work; travel; traveling ministry or work; to navigate; to be moved by the Spirit; to wonder.

Reference:Jdg 13:25; Hab 1:8

Large airplane – *Church:* Large ministry; travel.

Small airplane – *Person or personal ministry:* Small ministry; travel.

Airplane crash – *Sudden failure:* Personal disaster (i.e. failed business, failed marriage, etc.); ministry disaster; strife;

contention; calamity; difficulty; destruction or loss; to turn away from responsibility; mistake; failure; sin; desertion; rejection of faith and a good conscience. (Also see **Automobile Wreck, Car Crash, Boat/Shipwreck** and **Shipwreck**)

Reference:2 Chr 20:35-37; Acts 27; Rom 11:9-12; 2 Cor 11:25; 1 Tim 1:18-19.

Flying or soaring – *Overcoming:* To find new strength; conquer; to triumph over something; up in a direction; to raise; to elevate; to lift; to ascend; being moved by the Holy Spirit; soaring in the Spirit; to elevate the spirit; to be carried on wings; God our deliverer.

Reference:Num 13:30; Deut 30:12; 32:11-13; Ps 18:10; 139:8; Hab 1:8; Zech 5:1-4; Jn 16:33; 1 Jn 2:13; 4:4; 5:4-5.

Warplane – *Warrior:* Fighter; spiritual warfare; used in war or battle; kamikaze; to drop a bomb; to have a bomb dropped.

Reference:1 Chr 12:28; Jer 49:2; 50:9; Ezek 32:12; 2 Cor 10:4; 1 Tim 1:18; 2 Tim 2:4.

Airport – *Preparation:* Waiting; training; place of transition; readiness; to be ready; ready to go; travel; ministry; the church; place of opportunity; porthole (inlet or outlet); door or gate; terminal. (Also see Train Station and Bus Station)

Reference:Gen 19:1; 28:17; 1 Sam 7:3; Job 38:17; Ps 25:5,21; 27:14; Acts 1:4;17:16; Rom 8:25; Gal 5:5; Php 3:20; 1 Thes 1:10; Heb 9:28; 1 Pet 3:20.

Alabaster – *Container:* Fragrance contained within; perfume flask; white stone.

Reference:Est 1:6; Mt 26:7; Mk 14:3; Lk 7:37.

Alarm – *Warning:* Alert; SOS; call 911; warning signal; to warn of sudden danger; frighten; surprise; shock.

Reference:Num 10:1-10; Jdg 7:20-23; 2 Chr 13:12; Jer 4:19; 49:2; Joel 2:1; Zeph 1:16.

Alligator (or Crocodile) – *Ancient:* Very old; powerful; danger; destruction; evil spirit; thick-skinned; twisting; evil intent; leviathan; domineering; one who attacks with the mouth; a big mouth; verbal attack. (Also see **Leviathan**)

Reference:Job 41:1-10; Jer 51:34; Ezek 29:3, 32:2.

Altar – *Sacrifice:* A place of spiritual sacrifice; the place of atonement; a memorial; a place of prayer; a place of God's protection; a place of worship.

Reference:Gen 8:20; Ex 17:15; 20:24; 21:14; 30:1-10; Lk 1:10; Rom 12:1-2.

Amber – *The glory of God:* Fire; divine glory; glowing; brightness; shining light; God's glory in judgment; consuming fire; appearance of fire; purity; holiness; unapproachable presence of God.

Reference:Ezek 1:4, 27; 8:2; Acts 26:13; Heb 12:29; 1 Jn 1:5.

Amethyst – *Royalty:* Personal adornment; the Hebrew name means "dream stone"; known as the "sobriety stone"; used to curb one's passions, opinions, and appetites; to be of sound mind.

Reference:Ex 28:19, 39:12; Rev 21:20.

Anchor – *To hold fast:* To hold in place; to root in; to hold securely; steadfast; the promises of God.

Reference:Mk 6:53; Acts 27:29-30, 40; Heb 6:19.

Angel – *Messenger:* A message sent from God; actual angelic encounter.

Reference:Num 22:22-35; Lk 2:8-18; Heb 2:7; 13:2; 1 Pet 1:12; 3:22.

Ant – *Industrious:* Diligent; conscientious; tireless; wise; sticking to the task; wise in future preparations; foresight; industry; pestering; irritation; nuisance.

Reference:Pr 6:6-8; 10:5; 30:24-25.

Ape – *The uncivilized world*: Rough; intimidation; boaster; proud; clumsy; crude person; harsh; inferior quality; lack of civilized character; uncultivated; barbaric; brutish; wild; ill-bred; unrefined; unpolished; primitive; foolish; mischief; deceitful; not honest (as in "monkey business"); wickedness.

Reference:Neh 2:19; Ps 7:14-16; Pr 1:22; 2 Tim 3:1-7.

Apparel – Covering *(good or bad):* Christ's righteousness; purity; anointing; modesty; outward adornment.

Reference:1 Tim 2:9; 1 Pet 3:3.

Filthy garments – *Iniquity:* Unrighteousness; wickedness; vileness.

Reference:Isa 4:1-4; 64:6; Zech 3:3-7; Jas 2:2-4.

Clothes that don't fit – *Not equipped for service:* Walking in something you're not equipped for; operating outside your calling, something just doesn't fit; not prepared or ready; not adjusted to or shaped for; not correctly in place; not in agreement with; not properly equipped for service. (Also see Shoes/Shoes that don't fit)

New clothes – *New covering:* New beginnings; new blessings; new righteousness; new ministry; new gifts; new anointing; new spirit; new mantle; new covenant; fresh; change.

Reference:Gen 37:3-4; 45:22; Ezek 11:19-20; Mt 26:28; 2 Cor 3:18; 5:16-18; Heb 8:7-13; Jam 2:2-4; Rev 21:5.

Ark of the Covenant – *The presence of God:* God's law; mercy seat; the testimony of God; God's covenant, Yahweh's salvation and redemption; God's strength and protection; God's provision; God's holiness; place to know God's will; atonement.

Reference:Ex 25:13-22; 30:6, 36; Lev 16; Num 10:33; Josh 4:11; 1 Sam 3:3; 2 Chr 6:41; Jer 3:16-17; Rev 11:19.

Arm – *Strength:* Power; might; deliverance; protection; to rescue; saving; ruling; weakness.

Reference:Ex 6:6; Dt 7:19; Ps 44:3; 77:15; 89:10,13,21; Isa 53:1, 63:12; Jer 17:5; Lk 1:51; Jn 12:38; Acts 13:17.

Armor – *Protective covering:* Justice; defensive and offensive protection in warfare; complete spiritual covering; to protect oneself against the enemy; to fight against spiritual wickedness; equipped for battle; equipped with the full resources of God; God's justice.

Reference:Neh 4:16; Isa 59:17; 2 Chr 26:14; Jer 46:4; Eph 6:10-17; 1 Thess 5:8.

Belt – *Truth:* To hold tightly to; brace; to prepare; to gird up; to be invested with power and authority; to encircle with; to be enclosed; to surround; to bind.

Reference:1 Ki 18:46; 2 Ki 1:8; Ps 109:19; Isa 5:27; 11:5; 22:21; Mt 3:8; 1 Pet 1:13.

Breastplate – *Righteousness:* Offensive weapon; protection; Christ's righteousness; judgment; faith and love.

Reference:Ex 28:15; 29-30; Neh 4:16; Isa 59:17; Eph 6:14; 1 Thess 5:8.

Helmet – *Salvation:* Prepared; protection for thoughts; mind; saving power; promised; firm hope of salvation.

Reference:Isa 59:17; Jer 46:4; Ezek 23:24; Eph 6:17; 1 Thess 5:8.

Sandals – *Readiness:* Preparation of the gospel of peace; strength (also see, Shoes).

Reference:Dt 29:5; 33:25; Isa 5:27; Acts 12:8.

Shield – *Faith:* God our shield; protector; defense; favor; God our refuge.

Reference:Gen 15:1; Dt 33:29; 1 Sam 17:7,41; 2 Sam 22:3, 31, 36; Ps 3:3; 5:12; 8:2; 30:35, 28:7; 33:20; 35:2; 84:9; 89:18; 144:2.

Sword – *God's Word:* To cut to the very depths of the human heart; Scripture; Jesus Christ; God's judgment.

Reference:1 Sam 17:51; 1 Chr 21:12; Mt 10:34; 26:50-51; Rom 13:4; Eph 6:17; Heb 4:12; Rev 1:16; 13:10; 19:15, 21.

Arrow – *To penetrate deeply:* Words that go deep (good or bad); the Word of the Lord; the Lord's deliverance; to bear false witness against one's neighbor; to speak deceit.

Reference:2 Ki 13:17; Ps 11:2; 57:4; 64:7-8; Pr 25:18; Jer 9:8; Lam 3:12-13; Zech 9:14.

Art – *Creativity:* Creation; image; craft or crafted; craftsmanship; handiwork; creative imagination; the use of creative skills; the creation of beautiful objects; creativity; artistic talents and skills; man's devising; graven image; idols; idolatry; could be a symbol of an object being worshipped; manmade symbol of worship.

Reference:Gen 1:1; 1:26; 4:21-22; Ex 20:4; 30:25, 35; Lev 26:1; Isa 30:22; Jer 8:19; Acts 17:29.

Ashes – *Mourning:* Purification; repentance; victory; worthlessness; destruction.

Reference:Num 19:1-10; Est 4:1-3; Job 42:6; Jer 6:26; Ezek 28:18; Dan 9:3; Mal 4:3; Mt 11:21; Heb 9:13.

Attic – *Mind:* Think; thoughts; heart; attitudes; reasoning; imagination; opinion; belief; reason; intelligence; intellect; understanding; learning; affections; desires; will; memory; to remember. (Also see Elevator/Top floor, Stairs/Upstairs, Up/Upstairs, and Upper room)

Reference:Dt 18:6-7; 1Sam 2:35; 1Chr 22:7; Mt 22:37; Lk 12:29; Phil 3:13.

Automobile – *Person or ministry:* One's life; family (family in the family's car).

Automobile wreck: (See **Airplane/Airplane Crash**)

Convertible – *Covering or no covering:* Ability to be converted, exchangeable; changeable.

Reference.:Ps 51:13; Mt 18:2-3; Acts 3:19; 9:18.

With the top up – *Covering:* Shelter; refuge; atonement; mantle; covered by the glory of the Lord.

Reference:Ex 22:26-27; 24:16; Est 6:12; 1Sam 28:14; 2Ki 2:8-14; 19:1-2; Ps 91:9-11; 139:13; 140:7; Isa 4:5-6; Jon 4:5; Rom 4:7.

With the top down – *Uncovered:* Exposed (good or bad), revealed; to unlock; spiritual eyesight; vulnerable; to open; not protected.

Reference:Gen 9:21-23; 38:14-15; Pr 25:10; Ezek 16:22,36,39; Hos 2:3; Mk 7:34-35; Lk 12:2; 24:31; Jn 3:20-21; 1Cor 11:4-6; Eph 5:11-13.

Limousine – *Significant or having importance:* Status; social status; prestige; a mark of distinction; wealth; pride; arrogance.

Reference:Gen 41:43; Deut 20:1; 1Ki 4:26; Ps 20:7; Jer 51:21; Ezek 16:49; Mk 9:35.

New Car – *New ministry or new life:* New beginnings; new start; born again.

Reference:2Cor 5:17; Eph 2:15; Rev 21:5.

Old Car – *Old traditions:* Religiousness; relating to the past; outdated; worn out; needing revival; old wineskin.

Reference:Ps 119:83; Mt 9:17; 15:2-6; Mk 2:22; 7:3-9; Lk 5:37-38; Col 2:8.

Pickup Truck – *Work:* Personal ministry; natural work; powerful ministry; ability to carry the load.

Reference:1Chr 13:7; Gal 6:5

Van – *Family (church or natural):* Family ministry; fellowship.

Axe – *To cut down:* judgment; decision; divine authority; God's sovereignty; sudden termination; ruthless removal; chop or chopping; malicious destruction.

Reference: 1 Chron 20:3; Ps 74:5-7; Eccl 10:10; Isa 10:15, 33-34; Jer 10:3; 46:22; 51:20; Ezek 31:18; Dan 4:14,23; Mt 3:10; 7:19; Lk 13:6-9.

Sharp axe – *Wisdom.*

Reference: Eccl 10:10.

Dull axe – *Lacking intelligence:* Slow in perception; mentally slow; thick-headed; to lack intensity; half-witted.

Reference: Eccl 10:10.

B

Baby – *New:* New beginning; innocent; true believers; new Christians; natural baby; dependent upon; carnal Christians; offspring.

Reference:Ex 2:6; Ps 8:2; 17:14; Isa 3:4; Joel 2:16; Mt 11:25; 21:16; Rom 2:17-20; 1Cor 3:1; 14:20; 1Pet 2:2.

Back – *Past or previous:* Former; experience or event; memory; remember; recollection; learned from experience; revisit; go back or don't go back; unaware; unsuspecting.

Reference:Gen 19:26; 22:13; 24:20; Josh 8:4,26; Ps 6:10; Eccl 7:10; Isa 21:12; 28:6; 31:2; 42:9; Eph 4:22; Phil 3:13; Heb 10:38; 1Pet 1:14; Rev 21:4.

Baker – *One who cooks up something:* One who serves; to prepare; mover and shaker; instigator; to stir the pot; one who stirs up strife.

Reference:Gen 40:1-23; Hos 7:1-7.

Balm – *Healing:* To heal (as in "balm of Gilead"); healing of wounds; Jesus Christ (the Great Physician); medicinal; soothing ointment; to comfort or soothe.

Reference:Gen 37:25; Jer 8:22; 46:11; 51:8.

Bank – *Safe:* Secure; saved; treasures in heaven; money; a place for holding something; a deposit of something; storing our treasures in heaven; the church; storehouse; store away; set aside (as in "save for a rainy day").

Reference:Dt 28:8; Pr 3:10; Joel 1:17; Mal 3:10; Mt 6:20; 25:27; Lk 12:16-19; 18:22; 19:23.

Bankruptcy – *Destitute:* Unable to pay; debt; liquidation; lacking resources; financially ruined; sterile; destitute; depleted; lacking spiritually, emotionally, morally, or financially; lacking truth; lacking discernment.

Reference:Ps 34:10; 141:8; Pr 5:23; 10:21; 15:21; Ezek 4:16-17; 32:15; Lk 8:6; 12:21; 1Tim 6:5; Jas 2:15-16.

Banner – *Standard:* Christ; flag; signal; God's salvation, protection, and power; a sign; God's presence in times of need or help; "Jehovah-Nissi"; a call to assembly.

Reference:Ex 17:8-16; Num 2:2, 34; Ps 20:5; 60:4; 74:4-5; SS 2:4; 6:4-10; Isa 5:26; 11:10-12; 13:2; 18:3; 31:9; 62:10; Jer 51:27; Zech 9:16.

Banquet – *A lavish feast:* A ceremonial party or dinner; celebration of a special occasion or in honor of someone; the marriage supper of the Lamb; special preparation for; special garments; special seating.

Reference:Gen 29:22; 40:20; SS 2:4; Mt 8:11; Lk 13:29; 14:8-17; 15:22-25; Rev 19:17.

Barbershop: (See **Beauty Shop**)

Bar – *Worldly comforts:* The world; intoxicating carnal pleasures; carousing; harlotry; place of idolatrous worship; works of the flesh; counterfeit fellowship; spiritual outpouring (either good or bad); "son of" as in "Bar-Jonah" or "Son of Jonah"; to shut or keep out; to restrict; forbid; to prevent entry.

Reference:Neh 7:3; Job 38:10; Jer 13:13-14; Ezek 16:23-30; 23:33; Amos 1:5; Zech 12:2; Lk 21:34; Rom 13:12-13; Gal 5:18-21; 1Pet 4:3.

Barefoot – *Reverence:* A sign of great distress; forewarned of judgment; mourning; poverty.

Reference:Ex 3:5; 2Sam 15:30; Isa 20:2-4; Ezek 24:17-23; Lk 15:22.

Barn – *Storehouse:* A place of storage; church; heaven; God's blessing; works; supply; provision. (Also see Shed and Store)

Reference:Dt 28:8; Job 39:12; Ps 144:13; Pr 3:10; Joel 1:17; Hag 2:19; Mt 13:30; Lk 12:18-24.

Barren – *Unfruitful:* Inability to produce; unable to reproduce; inability to yield a harvest; lacking fruit; lack of power or strength; cursed; desolation; the grave (a barren womb); a judgment; lack of God's blessings.

Reference:Ex 23:26; Dt 7:14; 2Sam 6:23; Ps 107:34; 113:9; Pr 30:16; Joel 2:20; Lk 13:6-9.

Basement – *Soul:* Foundation; nature of the flesh; carnal; hidden; forgotten; secret sin; stored away; lust; foundation. (Also see Dungeon and Foundation)

Reference:Gen 40:15; Dt 32:22; Ez 3:10-13; Ps 11:3; 82:5; Pr 1:18; 21:14; Eccl 12:14; Isa 3:17; 19:10; 24:18; 45:3; Jer 38:6-13; Lam 3:53-55; Hab 3:13; Mk 4:22; Lk 6:48-49; Rom 8:6-8; 1Cor 3:1-15; 2Cor 10:4-6.

Bat – *Unclean:* Witchcraft; occult; deception; impure; fear; unaware (as in "blind as a bat"); living in dark places.

Reference:Lev 11:13-19; Dt 14:18.

Bath or Bathing – *Clean or cleansing:* To make clean; to wash; washing the body; to cleanse oneself; ceremonial cleansing; purification; to wash away the old and get ready for the new.

Reference:Ex 30:19-21; Lev 14:8; 2Ki 5:10-14; Est 2:12; Mk 7:2-3; Jn 13:10; 1Tim 5:10.

Bathroom – *Cleansing:* Repentance; to wash away the filth and wickedness; lust; hidden; secret sin.

Reference:2Sam 11:2,4; Ps 19:12; 51:10; Isa 1:16; Mt 8:3-4; Lk 8:17.

Beads – *Prayer:* Pray, to entreat; intercession; beauty; something precious; a jewel; pierced; to bore through; perforation; puncture; to run through.

Reference:SS 1:10; 4:9.

Bear – *Destruction:* Ferocious; fierce revenge; death; war; fool's folly; wicked rulers; cunning; danger; ambush; power; strong; destroyer; world empire; final antichrist; something in hibernation; Russia.

Reference:1Sam 17:34-37; 2Sam 17:8; Pr 17:12; 28:15; Lam 3:10; Dan 7:5-7; Hos 13:8; Rev 13:2.

Beard – *Respectability:* Trustworthiness; covering; old age; wisdom; low self-esteem (as in "to hide behind").

Reference:Lev 13:45; Ezra 9:3; Isa 7:20; 15:2; 50:6; Ezek 24:17; Mic 3:7.

> **Shaved beard** – *Mourning:* Trouble; shame; to put away filthiness; to clean; to put away the flesh.
>
> Reference:Num 8:7; Lev 13:45; 21:5; Ezra 9:3; Ezek 24:17.

Beauty Shop – *Preparation:* Church; vanity; righteousness; holiness; loveliness; to exalt the mind. (Also see Barbershop)

Reference:Ps 29:2; 49:14; Pr 31:30; Hos 10:5; 1Cor 11:15.

Beaver – *Diligent:* Industrious; busy; capable; clever; brilliant; ingenious.

Reference:Pr 10:4; 24:3.

Bed – *Rest:* Sleep; place of meditation and prayer; marriage; covenant; place of intimacy; safety; the Lord's support; self-made conditions (as in "you've made your bed, now sleep in it"); secret thoughts and words; hidden; comfort; illness; laziness; the grave; prostitution; covenant with the world; place of scheming; fornication; adultery. (Also see Couch)

Reference:Gen 49:33; 1Sam 3:3-4; 2Sam 4:5-7; Job 17:13-16; Ps 4:4; 36:4; 41:3; 63:6; Pr 7:16-17; 26:14; SS 3:1; Isa 57:7; Lk 11:7; Acts 9:34; Heb 13:4.

Bedroom – *Rest:* Intimacy; privacy; secrecy; peace; covenant; salvation; self-made conditions (as in "you've made your bed, now sleep in it"); secret thoughts and words; hidden; comfort; safety.

Reference:2Ki 6:12; 11:2; Ps 4:4; 149:5; Eccl 10:20; Isa 28:18-20; 57:2; Mic 2:1; Heb 13:4.

Bees – *Diligence:* Busy (as in "Busy as a bee"); industrious; diligent; to pollinate; stinging words; gossip; busybody; offense or resentment; affliction; pursuit; to drive out; threatening; surrounding, swarming. (Also see **Hornets** and **Wasps**)

Reference:Dt 1:44; Judg 14:8; Ps 118:12; Isa 7:18.

Belly – *Heart:* A person's true inner self; the place of one's carnal pleasures or worldly satisfactions; stomach; seat of affections (good or bad).

Reference:Jdg 3:21-22; Ps 17:14; Pr 18:20; 20:27,30; Rom 16:18; Phil 3:19.

Belt: (See **Armor/Belt**)

Bicycle – *Person or personal ministry:* Works (good or bad); labor; working out one's salvation; operating under one's own power; self-righteousness.

Reference:Eccl 2:11; Mt 9:37-38; Jn 4:38; 1Cor 15:58; Phil 2:16; Rev 3:8.

> **Tricycle** – *Training (good or bad):* Learning; disciple; equipping for ministry; growing and maturing in the Lord.
>
> Reference:Pr 22:6; Lk 6:40; Heb 12:11; 2Pet 2:14.

> **Two-Person Bike** – *Partnership:* Tandem; one behind another working together for a common purpose, team, agreement, union; marriage.
>
> Reference:Gen 2:18-25; 24:58; Ps 133:1; 2Chron 20:35-37; Ezek 37:17; Mt 19:5-6; Lk 5:10; 2Cor 8:23; Eph 5:22-24; Phm 17.

> **Stationary Bike** – *Vanity:* Going nowhere; labor; no profit; works; spinning your wheels.
>
> Reference:Eccl 2:11; Php 2:16.

Bible – *The Word of God:* The inspired and authoritative Word of God written by God through man as a testimony to Jesus and to bring guidance for salvation and life through Him. (Also see **Book**)

Reference:Ex 24:3-8; Ps 40:7; Jer 31:31-34; Lk 24:44-49; Heb 8:10; Rev 22:19.

Bird – *Spirit:* Holy Spirit; man; God's provision; demon; usually unclean; gossip; communication; spiritual messengers; to soar; to sing; to flee; to devour; scavengers.

Reference:Ps 11:1; 104:12; Eccl 10:20; Jer 4:25; Ezek 17:23; 31:6; Matt 6:26; 13:4,32; Jn 1:32; Rev 18:2; 19:17.

Bird Cage – *Trapped:* Bound; prison; prisoner; ensnared; snare; confinement for prisoners. (Also see **Cage, Dungeon,** and **Prison**)

Reference: Jer 5:26-27; Ezek 19:9; Rev 18:2.

Birth or Birthing – *Coming to life:* To bring forth life; the Word of God coming forth; pain forgotten; born again; to deliver; labor, pain, and suffering.

Reference:Gen 3:16; Ps 29:9; 48:6; Eccl 7:1; Isa 21:3; 37:3; 46:3; 66:7-9; Mic 4:10; 5:3; Mt 1:18-25; Jn 9:1; 16:21.

Black – *Sin:* Mourning; affliction; calamity; famine; death; grief; evil; hell; flesh; dim; gloomy; darkness; night; to be dirty; ignorance; humiliation; burned; tempest; sorrow; God's judgment.

Reference:Job 30:30; Pr 7:6-9; SS 1:5; 5:11; Jer 4:28; Lam 4:8; Mic 3:6; Zech 6:2; Mal 3:14; Heb 12:18; Jude 13; Rev 6:5.

Black Man or Black Woman – Could represent a specific person that you know; self; the characteristics of the man or woman may resemble someone you know; if he is a stranger. (Also see Black or Man/Kindly Stranger)

Reference:SS 1:5.

Black Panther – *Witchcraft:* Dangerous; destroyer; devourer; intimidation.

Reference:Ps 7:2; 10:9; Jer 2:30; 4:7; 49:19; Lam 3:10; 2Tim 4:17; 1Pet 5:8.

Blood – *Life of the flesh:* Covenant; redemption; sacrifice; lineage; kinship; impure; contaminated; polluted; unclean; wound; injury; death.

Reference:Gen 9:4-6; Lev 15:19; 17:11; Ps 106:38; Lk 22:20; 1Cor 11:25; Eph 1:7; 2:13.

Blue – *Divine revelation:* Heaven; heavenly authority; royalty; symbol of the revealed God; Holy Spirit; visitation; healing; reward; to remember the commandments of God; being holy for the Lord; sacred; depression; melancholy.

Reference:Ex 24:10; 28:31; Num 4:7,9; 15:38-40; Est 8:15; Ezek 1:26.

Black and Blue – *Bruise:* Injured; stripe; hurt; wounds; ruin; to pierce; smash; crush. (Also see Bruise)

Reference:Gen 3:15; Lev 22:24; Pr 20:30; Isa 30:26; 42:3; 53:5,10; Mt 12:20; Rom 16:20.

Boat – *Person or ministry:* Church; ministry of evangelism (as in "fishers of men").

Reference:Gen 6:16; Mt 4:19-22; 8:23-24; Mk 1:17-20; 4:1-2.

Powerboat – *Powerful ministry:* Fast progress.

Rowboat – *With hard labor:* Adversity.

Reference:Ps 107:23-30; Jonah 1:13; Mk 6:48.

Sailboat – *Moved by the Holy Spirit:* Reliance upon the wind of the Holy Spirit; difficulty; being tossed to and fro.

Reference:Ps 107:23-30; Mt 14:24-33; Acts 27; Eph 4:14; 2Pet 1:21.

Ship – *Large ministry:* Church; business.

Reference:Ps 107:23-30; Acts 27.

Shipwreck: (See **Airplane/Airplane Crash**)

Body – *Temple of the Holy Spirit:* Soul or spirit; instrument of righteousness or iniquity; spiritual unity of believers (church); God's image.

Reference:Gen 9:6; Pr 14:30; Mt 6:22-23; Rom 6:3-12; 12:4-5; 1Cor 6:19-20; 12:12-31; 15:40-44; Eph 4:4-16; 1Thess 5:23; Jas 2:26.

Bomb (Blown Up) – *To attack*: Sabotage; impact; explosive; snare; to undermine the progress of, forcibly moved, shatter, destroy, deliberate destruction, hindrance by the enemy, wreck; danger.

Reference:Ex 23:33; Job 16:12; Isa 8:9.

Book – *Word of God:* A set of writings bound together into a volume; printed narrative; literature; Bible; the Book of Life; a registry; journal; to record; wisdom; knowledge; revelation; intellect; scholastic; to study. (Also see Bible)

Reference:Ps 40:7; 56:8; Rev 20:12; 22:19.

Book on the shelf – *A Word that has not been drawn upon or utilized.*

Closed book – *Completion:* Conclusion; not open; enclosed; to bar passage; shut; end; to come to an agreement; finished.

Reference:Dan 12:8-9; Lk 4:20.

Open book – *Not secret or hidden:* Uncovered; not protected; free entry; free access; accessible; open opportunity; free from restraint; reveal; enlighten.

Reference:Ps 98:2; Isa 40:5; Neh 8:5; Dan 10:7; Lk 4:17; Rev 10:2, 8-10; 20:12.

Boomerang – *To return:* As you have done, it shall be done to you; recoil; opposite effect; to revert; to return; to turn back.

Reference:Oba 1:15

Bosom – *Heart:* Affection; cherished; inside; close; intimate; midst; within; connected; to recline upon; partaker of blessing; lap. (Also see Breast)

Reference:Gen 16:5; Ex 4:6; Num 11:12; Dt 28:54-56; 2Sam 12:3; Job 19:27; Pr 16:33; Lam 2:12; Jn 13:23-25.

Bowl – *Prayers of the saints:* A vessel; to hold (as in liquid or food); an outpouring of something such as spiritual blessings, judgments, God's wrath.

Reference:Eccl 12:6; Amos 6:6; Zech 4:2-14; Rev 5:8; 15:7; 16:1-17; 17:1.

Bracelet – *To adorn:* Beauty; royalty; worldliness.

Reference:Gen 24:22; Isa 3:18-19; Ezek 16:11.

> **Ankle bracelet** – *To draw attention to the wearer:* Self-glorification.
>
> Reference:Isa 3:18-21.

Branch – *Messiah:* Righteousness; Christians; descendant; Jew; Gentile (grafted).

Reference:Isa 4:2; 11:1; Jer 23:5-6; Zech 3:8; Jn 15:1-8; Rom 11:17-24.

Bread – *Christ:* Communion with Christ; Christ's body broken for His saints; food; life; strength; provision; increase; fellowship; adversity.

Reference:1Ki 17:6; 19:6; Ps 132:15; Isa 30:20-23; Lk 22:7-19; Jn 6:33-35; Acts 2:42-46; 20:11; 1Cor 10:17; 11:23-28.

Breast – *Care:* Wealth; blessing; supply; nourishment; nurturing; maturity; emotion and thought; pleasure; married love; lust; adultery; works of the flesh; lusts of the flesh; pornography. (Also see Bosom)

Reference:Gen 49:25; Ps 6:25; 22:9; Pr 5:19; Isa 60:16; SS 1:13; 4:5; Lam 4:3; Ezek 16:7; Hos 9:14; Mt 5:29; Lk 11:27; Rom 13:13; Gal 5:16-19; 2Pet 1:4; 1Jn 2:16-17.

Breath – *Life:* Alive; living; God's power; to take your breath = death; judgment.

Reference:Gen 2:7; Job 12:10; 37:10; Ps 104:29; 146:4; Eccl 3:19; Ezek 37:5-10; Dan 5:23; Jn 20:22; Acts 17:25; 2Thess 2:8.

Bride – *The Church:* Covenant; agreement; joined; virtuous; righteous; purity; chaste; Israel.

Reference:Isa 62:5; Ezek 16:8-14; Mt 9:15; 2Cor 11:2; Eph 5:25-33; Rev 21:2-9.

Bridegroom – *Jesus Christ:* Covenant; agreement; joined.

Reference:Ezek 16:8-14; Mt 9:15; 25:1-10; Jn 3:29.

Bridge – *Transition:* Difficult changes in life; to pass over (troubled or easy circumstances); to overcome obstacles; leaving the old and coming into the new.

Reference:Gen 31:21; 32:10; Dt 27:3-4; Josh 3:16-17; 4; Job 11:12-16; Mt 9:1; 14:34.

Standing at the entrance of the bridge – *Decision:* A place of decision making; to go forward or return from whence one came.

Reference:Josh 3:1; 1Chron 4:39; Est 5:1; 1Pet 1:11.

Brimstone (Sulfur) – *Barrenness or desolation:* Divine fire; judgment of God; God's wrath; future punishment of the wicked; burning; death; condition of hell.

Reference:Gen 19:24; Dt 29:23; Job 18:15; Ps 11:6; Isa 30:33; Ezek 38:22; Lk 17:29; Rev 9:17-18; 14:10; 20:10; 21:8.

Bronze (Brass) – *Strength:* Power; durability; firmness; obstinacy; endurance; Christ's glory; defensive weaponry.

Reference:Num 21:9; 2Chr 12:10; Job 6:12; 40:18; 41:27; Ps 107:16; Isa 45:2; 48:4; Jer 1:18; 15:20; Dan 10:6.

Brother – *Self:* Love of Christian believers for one another; brotherhood; spiritual or natural brother.

Reference:Mt 23:8; Acts 9:17; Rom 12:10; 14:10-15; 1Thess 4:6-9; Heb 13:1.

Brother-in-law – *Brother in Christ:* Fellow minister; partner; spiritual or natural brother-in-law; oneself; adversary.

Brown – *Flesh:* Dead; withered (dead grass); repentant; mortality; dark; dust of the ground (earth); mud; frailty of man; lacking a spirit; lacking joy; humanism.

Reference:Gen 2:7; 30:32-40; Ps 102:4-5; Isa 15:6; 40:6-8; Mt 13:6; Mk 4:6; Lk 10:11; Acts 13:51-52; 1Pet 1:24; Rev 8:7.

Bruise – *Surface wound:* Sin and moral decay; to inflict a wound; injury to flesh; to damage by force; disable; cripple; sacrificial death of Jesus for our iniquities. (Also see **Blue; Black & Blue**)

Reference:Gen 3:15; Lev 22:24; Pr 20:30; Isa 1:6; 30:26; 42:3; 53:5-10; Mt 12:20; Rom 16:20.

Building – *Nature of structure:* House; church; business; to build; construct; framework; established; stronghold.

Reference:2Sam 7:27; 1Ki 6:12; Lk 6:48; 1Cor 3:9; 2Cor 5:1; Eph 2:21.

Burning – *Cleansing:* To purge; cleansing; the presence of God (the burning bush); intense heat; passionate; test or trial; jealousy; punishment; God's wrath and anger; to consume with fire.

Reference:Gen 38:24; Ex 3:2-3; 27:20; 32:10-11; Dt 29:20-23; Ps 79:5; Isa 6:6-7; Dan 3:20-26; Lk 24:32.

Bus – *Church or large ministry involving many people:* Business; urban or community ministry; swiftness (greyhound).

Reference - Pr 30:29-31.

> **School bus** – *Teaching or equipping ministry:* Youth ministry; working with children; to nurture; training; learning; disciple.

Reference -Ps 127:3-5; Isa 40:10-11, 30-31; Mt 28:19-20.

Butterfly – *Freedom:* Release; liberty; transformed; renewing of the mind; fragile; beauty; flight; flighty.

Reference:Rom 12:2; 2Cor 3:18; 11:13.

    Caterpillar – *Devourer:* Potential; possibility; promise; develop; change. (Also see Locust and Grasshopper)

    Reference:Joel 1:4; Amos 4:9.

    Chrysalis – *Change:* Transformation; to make different; reshape; false apostle.

    Reference:Rom 12:2; 2Cor 3:18; 11:13.

    Moth – *Devourer:* Deterioration; destroyer; inner corruption; subtle; harmful to health or morals; rotten; foul smelling; God's judgments; without wisdom; the fading glory of man.

    Reference:Job 4:19; 13:28; Isa 50:9; Hos 5:12; Mt 6:19-21; Lk 12:33.

Buzzard: (See Vulture).

C

Cage – *Trapped:* Bound; prison; prisoner; ensnared; snare; confinement for prisoners. (Also see **Bird Cage, Dungeon** and **Prison**)

Reference:Jer 5:26-27; Ezek 19:9; Rev 18:2.

Cafeteria – *Service:* Church; work; serving or being served; teaching; learning; eating or feeding on the Word of God; helps. (Also see Kitchen)

Reference:Mt 25:35.

Camel – *Endurance:* Ability to withstand hardship; duration; fortitude; long journey; burden-bearer; endurance; swift; docile; servant; extraordinary wealth.

Reference:Gen 24:10-11, 32-35; Jer 2:23; 49:29-32; Mt 10:25; Lk 18:25.

Candle – *Light:* Lamp; Holy Spirit; the spirit of man; light in the darkness; God's law; God's Word; to illuminate; revelation; to guide; to make vision possible; to radiate; a source of light; enlightenment; truth; knowledge; understanding; life (short lived).

Reference:2Sam 22:29; Job 12:5; 18:5-6; 21:17,19; Ps 18:28; 119:105; Pr 6:23; 13:9; 20:20,27; 119:10; Mt 5:15-16; 25:1-13; Lk 8:16; Jn 5:35; Jas 2:26.

Candlestick (or Lampstand) – *Light in the darkness:* The life-giving power of God; God enlightening us; the church; to give light; to illuminate; the smallest light can dispel the greatest darkness.

Reference:Ex 25:31-39; 27:20-21; 30:8; Num 8:1-4; 1Sam 3:2-3; Zech 4:2,11; Mt 5:15; Mk 4:21; Rev 1:12-13,20; 2:5: 11:4.

Captain – *Civil or military official:* Jesus Christ; one who keeps order; the one in charge; authority; overseer; ruler.

Reference:Josh 5:14; 10-24; Jdg 11:6; 1Sam 8:12; Pr 6:7; Acts 28:16; Heb 2:10; 2Tim 2:4.

Car Crash – *Conflict:* Fight; struggle; personal disaster (i.e. failed business, failed marriage, etc.); strife; ministry disaster; difficulty; destruction or loss; to turn away from responsibility; desertion. (Also see **Airplane Crash** and **Shipwreck**)

Reference:2Chron 20:35-37; Acts 27; Rom 11:11-12; 2Cor 7:5; 11:25; 1Thess 2:2; 1Tim 1:18-19.

Carnival – *Worldly:* Exhibit; exhibitionism; divination; fortune-telling; carousing; covetous practices; to parade oneself; to attract attention to oneself; deception.

Reference:Luke 21:34; Act 16:16; 2Pet 1:13-14.

Carpenter – *Builder:* Skilled craftsman; master builder = Christ; one who builds; laborer; preacher.

Reference:2Ki 22:6; Isa 28:17; 41:7; Zech 4:10; Mk 6:3; 1Cor 3:9.

Carpet (or Rug) – *Covering:* The covering of the foundation; something we stand on; to place underneath or below; to spread out; outer garment; mantle; to sweep it under the rug; to cover something up.

Reference:2Sam 17:19; Ps 105:39; Isa 25:7; 28:20; Mk 4:22; 2Cor 4:2.

Cartoon Character – *Characteristics of a person:* Someone who acts like or resembles the characteristics of the cartoon character; humorously distorted; satire; spoof; caricature; distorted representation; to produce a ridiculous effect.

Castle (or Palace) – *Kingdom (God's or man's):* Fortress; bearing dignity or grandeur; impressive; majestic; dwelling; implying authority; to establish by force; church; a government; fortress; storehouse; lofty and proud; stronghold; contentions.

Reference:Num 31:10; 1Chr 11:5-7; 27:25; 2Chr 17:12; 27:4; Ps 45:15; Pr 18:19; 30:28; Isa 25:2; Nah 2:6; Mt 5:3; Lk 11:21.

Cat – *Self-willed:* Spiteful; not trainable; stealthy; crafty; deception; unclean spirit; fascinating and bewitching and irresistible charm (witchcraft); sensuality; slanderous; sleek, lying in wait. (Also see **Leopard** and **Lion**)

Reference:Job 5:12; Ps 10:1-2; 83:3; Pr 6:25; 7:10-12,21; Lk 11:53-54; 2Cor 12:16.

Kitten – *Immaturity:* Young; new believers; precious; to nourish.

Reference:Judg 14:5-6; Job 4:11; Jer 2:15; Ezek 19:2-5; Nah 2:12.

Personal pet = something dear and of great value; near to one's heart; beloved.

Reference:Pr 7:10-12,21.

Cave – *Refuge:* Protection; habitation; to hide; secret; out of sight; temporary dwelling places; burial; a hollow place.

Reference:Gen 19:30; Josh 10:16-27; 1Sam 22:1; 1Ki 18:4; Isa 2:19; Jn 11:38; Rev 6:15.

Chaff – *Worthless:* Debris; the ungodly; emptiness; separated; false doctrine; God's judgment; punishment; to ridicule; mock. (See also Hay and Straw)

Reference:Ps 1:4; 35:5; 83:13; Isa 17:13; 33:11; Jer 23:28; Mt 3:12.

Chains – *Bondage:* Covenant bond; confinement; oppression; to restrain movement; held as a prisoner; bonds of sin and wickedness; everlasting punishment.

Reference:Jdg 15:14; Ps 68:6; 105:18; 149:8; Isa 58:6; Jer 40:4; Ezek 20:37; Acts 12:6-7; 21:33; 26:29; 28:20; Eph 6:20; 2Tim 1:16; 2Pet 2:4; Jude 6-7; Rev 20:1.

Chair – *Position:* Place of power or authority; dignity; throne; an official seat; chairman or chairperson; to act as an official over something; preside; relaxation; rest; fellowship or socializing; place of judgment. (Also see Seat)

Reference:1Ki 10:19; 2Ki 4:10; Ps 9:4,7; 11:4; 45:6; 122:5; Pr 9:14; Isa 16:5; Acts 7:49; Rev 3:21; 4:2; 13:2; 18:7.

Chariot – *Vehicle of war:* Symbol of dominion or superiority; command or rulership; military valor and skill; extraordinary ability.

Reference:Ex 14:6-9,25; 2Ki 2:11-12; Ps 20:7; 46:9; 68:17; 104:3; Isa 66:15; Jer 46:9; Joel 2:5; Nah 2:3-4: 3:2; Zech 6:1-8; Rev 9:9.

Cheek – *Humility:* Beauty; reproach; disapproval; rebuke; disgrace; to insult; offense.

Reference:Job 16:10; Ps 3:7; SS 5:13; Lam 3:30; Mic 5:1; Mt 5:39; Lk 6:29.

Cheetah: (See Leopard)

Chicken – *Provision:* Arise and shine (as in "cock-a-doodle-doo"); mothering; denial; coward; fear; lacking courage.

Reference:1Ki 4:23; Isa 60:8; Mt 26:34,74; Mk 13:35; 14:30; Lk 22:34; Jn 18:27.

Hen – *Gatherer:* Mothering; protector; gossip.

Reference:Mt 23:37; Lk 13:34.

Rooster (Cock) – *Arise and shine:* Watch; alert; to make aware of; attentive; signal; SOS; proud; arrogant; boasting; bragging; display; look; wake up; be ready and alert; leader (as in "to rule the roost").

Reference:Mt 26:34,74; Mk 13:35; 14:30, 68-72.

Childbirth: (See Birth or Birthing)

Children – *God's own:* Christians; disciples; church; God's gifts; heritage; descendents; devil's own; the crown of old men; playful; come to Christ as children; faith of a child; training; spiritual growth; childlikeness.

Reference:Gen 33:5; Dt 30:2; 1Sam 1:22; Ps 127:3-5; Pr 17:6; Mk 10:24; Rom 8:16-17; Gal 4:1-3; Eph 5:8; 6:1-4; 1Pet 2:2; 1Jn 3:10.

Illegitimate children – *Rejected:* No inheritance; fatherless or motherless; not part of God's kingdom; despised.

Reference:Dt 23:2; Judg 11:2; Gal 4:30; Heb 12:8.

One's own children - *Oneself or themselves:* Gifts; training; discipline; nourishment; instruction; inheritance; heritage; obedience; honor parents.

Reference:Gen 25:27; 33:5; 1Sam 1:22; 1Ki 15:11,26; Ps 127:3-5; Mt 18:6; Mk 10:13-16; Gal 4:1-2; Eph 6:1-4; Heb 12:9.

Orphan – *Fatherless and motherless:* No inheritance; grief; helpless; trouble; God's mercy.

Reference:Ex 22:22-23; Dt 10:18; 14:29; Ps 10:14-18; 146:9; Isa 1:17; Hos 14:3; Jas 1:27.

Choker – *To choke:* To choke the Word; to hinder; unfruitfulness; deceitfulness of riches.

Reference:Mt 13:22; Mk 4:19; Lk 8:14.

Church Building – *Church:* Assembly; congregation; the body of Christ; religious community; fellowship of the saints; the bride of Christ; habitation for the Holy Spirit.

Reference:Mt 16:18; Acts 11:26; 1Cor 12:18-24; Eph 2:22; 3:9,21; 5:22-32; Rev 19:7.

Circle – *Unity:* A group bound by a common tie; marriage; tightly knit together; in the crowd; peace; to move in a circle; eternity; wheel; to revolve; to surround; to protect.

Reference:Jos 6:11; 2Sam 5:23; 1Chr 14:14; Ps 133:1; Mark 3:34; Eph 4.

Semi-circle – *not complete:* Not in complete unity; not knit together; dissension; disunity; division.

Reference:Acts 15:2; 23:7-12.

City – *Characteristic by which the city is known for:* (EXAMPLE: RENO – gambling; prostitution; risky, etc.); characteristic of a person; the church; place where people dwell on a permanent basis; political entity; stronghold.

Reference:1Sam 20:40; 2Sam 5:7; Ezek 11:23; Jude 7.

Clay – *Building:* Vessel; impure mixtures; perishable; mortal human body; frailty of man's flesh; weakness of man; unstable kingdom; malleable or moldable; capable of being shaped; adaptable; pliable; the craftsmanship of God.

Reference:Job 4:19; 10:9; 13:12; Ps 40:2; 69:14; Isa 64:8; Jer 38:6; Dan 2:33-45; Rom 9:21-23.

Clock or Watch – *Watch:* It's time; times and seasons; seconds, minutes, or hours; days, weeks, months, years, decades, centuries, or millennia; get ready; be prepared.

Reference:2Ki 20:9-11; Isa 38:8; Mk 13:33-35; Lk 12:38-40; Eph 1:10; 2Pet 3:8-9.

Closet – *Private:* Personal; prayer closet; secret sin; hidden.

Reference:Ps 91:1; Mt 6:6; Mk 4:22; Lk 8:17.

Clouds – *Promise:* Showing the power and wisdom of God; divine presence; to pour out or hold back; dust beneath His feet; heavenly transportation; guidance; armies or multitudes of people; wiping out of transgressions; God's strength; God's judgment.

Reference:Ex 16:10; 40:34-38; 1Sam 12:17-18; 1Ki 18:44-45; Job 37:10-12; 38:34-37; Ps 135:6-7; 68:4; Pr 3:20; 25:14; Isa 19:1; 44:22; 60:8; Jer 4:13; Ezek 30:3; 34:12; Dan 7:13; Nah 1:3; Mt 24:30; 2Pet 2:17; Jude 12; Rev 1:7.

Clouds without water – *False Teachers.*

Reference:2Pet 2:17; Jude 12.

Pillar of cloud and fire – *The Lord going before:* To lead and guide; miraculous origin; supernatural; sign and wonder; the visible representation of the invisible God; the zeal of the Lord; destruction against rebellion.

Reference:Ex 13:18-22; 14:24, 19; 16:10; 40:34-38; Num 14:14; 16:35; Lev 10:2; Neh 9:12-19; Isa 4:4-5.

Clown – *Fool:* Foolishness; to entertain; jester; mocker; hypocrite; entertainer; to seek public applause rather than divine approval; man pleasing; self-glorification; to draw attention to oneself.

Reference:Ps 35:16; Pr 10:23; Eccl 2:2; 7:4.

Coal – *Purification:* To overcome evil; to burn inwardly; to purge; fuel; lust; God's judgment.

Reference:Job 41:21; Ps 11:6; 18:12-13; Pr 6:25-28; Isa 6:6; 54:16; Rom 12:20.

Coat (Cloak) – *Mantle:* Covering; protection; to envelope; to conceal; devotion; outer garment; zeal; piety; devoutness to religion. (Also see Robe)

Reference:Gen 37:3; Isa 59:17; Mt 23:5; 1Pet 2:16.

Cockroach – *Infestation:* Nuisance; unclean spirit; hidden sin; filthiness.

Reference:Job 15:16; Pr 30:12; 2Cor 7:1; Col 3:8; Jam 1:21.

Computer – *Manmade or worldly insight:* Instrument of modern technology; electronic processing; information processing;

programmable; to store and process data; analytical; workstation; input or output device; information; worldly knowledge; artificial intelligence.

Couch – *Resting place:* To sit; to lie down; to be at ease; laziness (as in "couch-potato"); a place of scheming. (Also see **Bed**)

Reference:Job 7:13; Ps 6:6; 36:4; Pr 26:14; Ezek 23:41; Amos 3:12; Lk 5:18.

Cougar – *Wild:* Powerful; stealthy; crafty; deception; false ministers; treacherous; imposter; unclean spirit. (Also see **Wolf**)

Reference:Job 5:12; Ps 7:14; 83:3; 119:78; Mt 7:15; 24:24; 2Cor 11:12-16; Gal 2:4; 2Tim 3:13; 2Pet 2:1; 1Jn 4:1.

Country – *Peaceful:* Isolated; separated; privacy; quiet; restful; removed; leisure; land; soil. (Also see Farm)

Reference:Ps 55:6-7; Pr 25:25; Isa 1:7; Mk 6:31; Heb 11:9-16.

Courthouse – *Justice:* Judgment; trial; legal matter; persecution; guilty or innocent; witness (true or false); to testify; testimony (true or false); accuser; accusation; controversy; punishment; conviction; sentence of judgment. (Also see Judge and Lawyer)

Reference:Dt 16:18-19; 17:6-13; 19:15-21; Jdg 4:5; Job 9:19; Ps 94:15-20; Isa 43:12; Mt 18:15-19; 26:59-62; Mk 15:3-5; 1Cor 6:1.

Cow – *Provision:* A rebellious woman; backsliding; provision; fat; well-fed; female; false prophetess; vixen. (Also see **Cow/Ox**)

Reference:Lev 22:27-29; Isa 7:21-22; Ezek 4:15; Hos 4:16; Amos 4:1.

Bull – *Expectation of increase* (as in "a bull market"): Male; decree; nonsense; spiritual; warfare; strength; opposition; slander; accusation; persecution; evil men; mighty men.

Reference:Lev 22:27-29; Dt 33:17; Ps 22:12; 68:30; Isa 34:6-7; Heb 9:13; 10:4.

Calf – *Increase:* Prosperity; sacrifice; sanctified saints; prayers; praise; thanksgiving; false worship; idolatry; stubbornness; materialism.

Reference:Lev 22:27-29; Hos 4:16; 13:2,5; Mal 4:2; Col 3:5; Heb 13:15.

Cattle – *Prosperity:* Possession; ownership; occupancy; property; something owned; title. (Also see **Sheep** and **Goats**)

Reference:Ps 50:10; 107:38; Jn 4:12.

Cud - *Remember:* Chewed again; ponder; reason; thinking; rethinking; meditate; consider; mull over; continuing; reflect upon; remember; memory; remind; recall; bring back to mind what is lost or scattered; clean or unclean.

Reference:Lev 11:3; Num 5:15; Ps 22:27-28; 63:5-6; 77:6; Eccl 1:11; Isa 43:26; Jn 14:26; 2Tim 1:5.

Ox – *Sacrifice:* Strength; wild and ferocious; servant labor; Christ; apostles; disciples; burden bearing; to give oneself sacrificially. (Also see **Cow**)

Reference:Num 7:88; Ps 22:12; 144:17; Pr 14:4; 1Cor 9:9; 1Tim 5:18.

Crimson – *Wealth:* Veil; curtain; shield; lips; sin.

Reference:2Sam 1:24; 2Chr 3:14; Pr 31:21; SS 4:3; Isa 1:15-18; Jer 4:30; Rev 17:4.

Crooked – *Spiritually distorted:* Perverse; twisted; dishonest; evil; darkness; wicked; iniquity. (Also see Leviathan)

Reference:Dt 32:5; Ps 125:5; Pr 2:12-15; Eccl 1:15; Isa 27:1; 40:3-4; Lk 3:4-5; Phil 2:14-15.

Crops – *Sowing and reaping:* Yield at harvest; reaping what you sow; fruits of your labor; reward of righteousness or wickedness; spiritual labors; harvest of a land.

Reference:Ex 9:32; Pr 22:8; Hos 8:7; 10:12-13; Mt 13:8,26; 1Cor 9:11; Gal 6:8-9.

Corn – *Seed:* Life coming through death; Christ's death producing much fruit for the harvest. (Also see Crops/Wheat)

Reference:Gen 1:11-12; Eccl 11:6; Mt 13:8,26; Jn 12:24; 2Cor 9:10; Gal 6:8-9.

> **Hay** – *Worthless:* Perishable; man's works; to bundle; flesh; stubble. (See also Chaff, Grass, and Straw)
>
> Reference:Isa 5:24; 33:11; 1Cor 3:12-13; 1Pet 1:24.

> **Straw** – *Worthless:* Threshed; chaff; dross; crushed; shredded; pulverized; trampled; stubble; perishable. (Also see Chaff and Hay)
>
> Reference:Ex 5:7-18; Job 21:18; 41:27-29; Isa 25:10; 1Cor 3:12-13.

> **Wheat** – *Harvest:* Seed; life coming through death; Christ's death producing much fruit for the harvest; threshing; spiritual blessing; Christians; bread; resurrection. (Also see Crops/Corn)

Reference:Jdg 6:11; Ruth 2:23; Ps 81:16; Mt 3:12; 13:24-30; Jn 12:24; 1Cor 15:37.

Cross – *The power of God:* Grace given to His saints through Christ; Christ's sufferings; our duty as Christians; civil and military public punishment; sinless sacrifice for our iniquities.

Reference:Deut 21:22-23; Mt 10:38; 16:24; Mk 8:34; Lk 9:23; 1Cor 1:17-18; Gal 6:14-15; Eph 2:16.

Crow/Raven – *Gloat:* Brag; boast; accomplishments (toot one's own horn); outspoken; confusion; humiliation; hateful; strife; unclean; direction (as in "as the crow flies"); demonic power.

Reference:Lev 13:15; Ps 35:26; Pr 30:17; Isa 34:11; Jas 3:16.

Crown – *Symbol of glory:* Glory and honor; Christ; the church; the Christian's reward; a good wife; old age; grandchildren.

Reference:Pr 12:4; 16:31; 17:6; Isa 62:3; 1Cor 9:25; 2Tim 2:5; Heb 2:7-9; Jas 1:12.

Crystal – *Wisdom:* Clear; transparent; gates of Zion; descriptive of heaven; holiness and purity (as in the Sea of Glass). (Also see Glass)

Reference:Job 28:17-20; Isa 54:12; Rev 4:6.

Cup – *One's portion:* To drink; blessings; consolation; suffering; the new covenant; endurance of suffering; hypocrisy; everlasting punishment of the wicked; the Lord's wrath.

Reference:2Sam 12:3; 1Ki 10:21; Ps 11:6; 23:5; 75:8; Isa 51:17-22; Jer 16:7; 49:12; Ezek 23:31-32; Mt 10:42; 20:22-23; 23:25-26; 26:39; Lk 11:39; Jn 18:11; 1Cor 10:16; 11:25; Rev 14:10; 17:4.

Curtain: (See **Veil**)

D

Dancing – *Worship:* Rejoicing in the Lord; time of rejoicing; joy; emotional expression; celebration of a joyous occasion; the opposite of mourning; exhibition of lust.

Reference:2Sam 6:14-16; 1Chr 15:25-29; Ps 30:11; 149:3; 150:4; Eccl 3:4; Mt 14:6; Mk 6:22.

Darkness – *Containing no light:* Outside the presence of God; unfruitful works; affliction; moral depravity; ignorance and unbelief; chaos; evil; death; hell; everlasting punishment of the wicked.

Reference:Gen 1:2; Job 10:21-22; 17:12; 21:17; 24:13-17; Ps 112:4; Mt 22:13; Jn 1:5; 3:19-20; Rom 13:12; Eph 5:11; Col 1:13; 2Pet 2:17; Rev 16:10; 18:23.

Daughter: (See **Children/One's Own Children**)

Day – *Light:* Morning; time period; happiness; knowledge; truth; enlighten; shine; clear; sun; life.

Reference:Gen 1:3-5; Num 8:2; Ps 56:13; 89:15-16; Isa 5:20; 30:26; Mic 7:8.

Death – *The consequence of sin:* Repentance; to die to the flesh; the act of terminating; repentance; conclusion; to finish; stop; physical death; the grave; loss; sorrow; mourning.

Reference:1Sam 2:6; Ps 23:4; Isa 26:14; 57:1-2; Jn 12:24; Rom 5:12-21; 1Cor 15:31; Phil 1:20-21; Heb 2:14; 9:27.

Deer – *Graceful:* Swift; quick on one's feet; agile; timid and shy; alert; a good wife; sure-footed.

Reference:1Chr 12:8; 2Sam 22:34; Ps 42:1; Pr 5:19; Isa 13:14; 35:6; Hab 3:19.

Buck (Roe) – *Power:* Royal; rule; kingly; strive; swift; protect; instincts; ornament; glory; glorious; goodly; pleasant.

Reference:SS 2:7,17; 1Chr 12:8.

Horns – *Authority:* God's power; exaltation; call; proclamation; announcement; alarm; strength and honor; power; attack and defense; destruction; salvation; anointing; revival; exalting; pride and arrogance (tooting one's own horn); to boast; conquest.

Reference:Dt 33:17; 1Sam 2:1,10; 1Ki 22:11; Ps 18:2; 75:4-10; Jer 48:25; Dan 7:7-8,21; Hab 3:4; Zech 1:18-21; Lk 1:69.

Demon – *Unclean spirit:* Not of God; evil spirit; one who instigates deceit; to be judged; satan's angels; one who inflicts suffering upon man.

Reference:1Ki 22:21-23; Mt 8:28-29; 10:1; 12:24-30; 25:41; Mk 5:1-5; Lk 10:17-18; 1Tim 4:1; 2Pet 2:4; Jude 6.

Den – *Hideout:* Secret sin; hidden; private; hiding place; dwelling place; asylum; cave; pit; retreat; refuge; stronghold.

Reference:Jdg 6:2; Ps 10:9; 104:22; Jer 7:11; Dan 6:7-24; Mt 21:13; Mk 11:17; Lk 19:46; Heb 11:38.

Desert – *Wilderness:* A place of temptation; that which is dry and thirsty; barren; wasteland; depressed; dryness; desolation; solitary place; a place of privacy and prayer with the Father.

Reference:Ps 78:40; 106:14-15; Is 21:1; 35:1-10; 40:3; 43:19-20; 48:21; Ezek 13:4; Joel 1:19-20; Lk 4:42; Jn 6:31.

Dew – *Blessing of God:* Refreshing; revive; beneficent power of God; moisture; speech; brotherly love and unity; purify.

Reference:Gen 27:28,39; Ex 16:13-14; Dt 32:2; 33:13,28; Ps 133:3; Pr 19:12; Hos 14:5.

Diamond – *Invincible:* Hard; to overcome; durability; brilliant; giving much light; pure; gift; sacred; precious; hardheaded; hard-hearted; stubborn will; rebellious. (Also see Flint)

Reference:Pr 17:8; Isa 50:7; Jer 17:1; Ezek 3:8-9; 28:13; Zech 7:12.

Dining Room – *Eat:* Fast or break one's fast; meditate upon the Word of God; eat the "spoil of your enemies"; love; fellowship; hospitality and service; the marriage supper of the Lamb.

Reference:Gen 43:16; Dt 20:14; Pr 15:17; Jer 15:16; Ezek 3:1-3; Mt 22:4; Lk 14:12-14; Rev 10:9-10.

Dinosaur – *Ancient:* Extinct; no longer active; old religious doctrine; long time past; an aged person; old fashioned.

Dirt – *Used for planting:* Soil (good or bad); involved in the harvest process; grief and mourning; flesh; despised; filth; pollution; sin; iniquity; depravity; defilement; wickedness; to be dirty; impure.

Reference: 2Sam 22:43; Ps 18:42; Isa 28:24; 57:20; 64:6; Ezek 17:8; 2Chr 26:10; Jn 9:6.

Ditch – *Trouble:* Pit; trap of falsehoods; snare of the enemy; false accusers fall into the ditch which they have made; wicked fall into; blind leaders fall into; the works of a harlot and a seductress.

Reference:Ps 7:14-17; 9:15; 35:7-8; 57:6; Pr 23:27; 26:27; 28:10; Mt 15:14; Lk 6:39.

Divorce – *To divide:* To separate; to break covenant; to leave.

Reference:Mal 2:14-16; Mt 5:31; Mk 10:2-9; Rom 7:2-3.

Doctor – *Healer:* One skilled in healing; restorer; repairer; recovery of health; Jesus Christ; the Holy Spirit; to give medical treatment to; medical doctor.

Reference:2Chr 16:12; Jer 8;22; Mt 9:12; Mk 2:17; 5:26; Lk 4:23.

Dog – *Contention:* Guide; guardian; strife; offense; unclean; unbelievers; evil workers; disobedient; covetous; boasters; hypocrites; proud; disobedient; fierce; foolishness; worthless; contemptible; promiscuity; hypocrite; false teachers.

Reference:Ex 11:7; Dt 23:18; 1Sam 17:43; 24:14; 2Sam 9:8; 16:9; Ps 59:6,14; Pr 26:11-17; Isa 56:10; Mt 7:6; 15:26-27; Gal 5:15; 2Pet 2:22; 2Tim 3:2-4; Rev 22:15.

Barking – *Warning:* Alarm; signal; summons; put on guard; watchmen; caution; inform; keep away; annoyance; nuisance.

Reference:Isa 52:8; 56:10; 62:6; Joel 2:1; Acts 16:18.

Biting pet – *Betrayal:* Seduce; to prove unfaithful; to reveal unintentionally; double cross; sell out; stab in the back (as in "forty pieces of silver"); betrayal; leak; expose; uncover; creditors; to be consumed; to devour one another.

Reference:Mic 3:5; Hab 2:7; Gal 5:15.

Bulldog – *Tenacious:* Protector; dangerous; stubborn; inflexible; rigid. (Also, Doberman or Rottweiler).

Reference:Jdg 2:19.

Hound – *Hunter:* Persistent; to pursue relentlessly; irritation; repeated annoyance; drive up the wall; obsession; sensitive to the things that are hidden (scent); driving those things that are hidden out into the open.

Reference:Ps 51:6; 56:2; Jer 20:16; 26:3; Dan 2:22; Zech 8:14; Mt 10:26-28.

Personal pet – *Friend:* Something dear and of great value; near to one's heart; beloved (as in man's best friend).

Reference:Ps 15:3-5.

Tucked tail – *Fear:* Coward; lacking courage; timidity; guilt; wrongdoing; shame.

Reference:Ps 35:4,26; 70:3; Pr 11:2; Jer 47:3; 2Tim 1:7; Heb 10:38-39.

Wagging tail (Waggish) – *Friendly:* Happy, joy; acceptance; accepting truth; frolicsome; full of merrymaking; pleasure; delightful; full of high spirits.

Reference:2Chr 17:6; Job 22:26; Ps 1:2; 16:11; 37:4,11; SS 2:3; Isa 11:3.

Watchdog – *Protection:* Guard; intercessor; watchman; alert; defensive position; defending; patrol.

Reference:2Sam 18:24-27; Is 21:5-6,11-12; 56:10; 62:6; Jer 6:17; Ezek 3:17; 33:6-7; Mt 24:42-43.

Door – *Entrance:* Opportunity; opening; Jesus Christ; the day of salvation; hope; faith; readiness. (Also see **Gate, Gateway, Portal,** or **Window**)

Reference:Hos 2:15; Mt 25:10; Lk 13:24-25; Jn 10:7-9; Acts 5:19; 14:27; 1Cor 16:9; 2Cor 2:12; Rev 3:7-8.

Dove – *Holy Spirit:* Advocate of peace; peaceful policy; loveliness; harmlessness; antiwar; reconciliation; undefiled; with God (Gen 8:8-12); peace; disposition; tender and devoted; affection; (Song 1:15; 2:14); mourning (Isa 38:14; 59:11); gentleness; sacrifice. (Also **Pelican** and **Turtledove**)

Reference:Lev 1:14-17; SS 2:14; Mt 3:16; 10:16; Jn 1:32.

Down – *Spiritually declined:* Backslide; to fall away; humble; prostrate; shame; to descend; to descend from heaven; to overcome or be overcome.

Reference:Gen 12:10; Job 33:24-28; Ps 30:3; Pr 14:14; Isa 14:12-13; 25:10-12; Jer 3:25; 6:15; Lk 10:15,30; Jn 6:51,58; Acts 7:34; Rom 10:6; 2Cor 10:4-5; Heb 11:30; Rev 3:21; 5:8.

Downstairs – *Demotion:* Decline; to go down; spiritual decline; backsliding; stubborn; faithless; old life of sin and idolatry; failure.

Reference:Dt 21:18-20; 1Sam 15:23; 2Chr 28:19; Ps 78:8; 81:12; Pr 14:14; Jer 3:6-22; 8:5; 31:22; Hos 4:16.

Dragon - (or Crocodile) – *satan:* Antichrist; danger; destruction; deception; evil spirit; wicked; ancient; powerful; forces opposed to God; demon; wolf.

Reference:Ps 91:13; 104:26; Isa 27:1; 51:9; Jer 51:34; Ezek 29:3; Rev 12:3-17; 13:2-11.

Dress – *Modesty:* To be presentable; to prepare for something; to cover.

Reference:2Sam 19:24; 2Chr 28:15; Est 5:4-12; Ps 147:8; Joel 2:16; Mt 22:11-14; 25:36; 2Tim 2:21; 1Pet 3:1-6.

Drowning – *Overcome:* Overwhelmed; to be under the circumstances; depression; oppression; temptation.

Driver – *Control:* Director of motion; steersman; foreman; overseer; manager; ministry leader; pastor; teacher; self; Christ; those responsible for getting a job done. (Also see Pilot)

Reference:Gen 39:4-5; Dt 9:5; 1Ki 22:34; 2Ki 9:20; Neh 11:9; Pr 16:26; Isa 44:25; Acts 20:28; Titus 1:7; 1Pet 2:25.

Drugs – *Intoxicant:* Under the influence of; to influence; mind-altering substance; medicine; healing; addiction; dependency; controlled substance; spell-giving potion; sorcery; witchcraft; great potency; to fight off what ails you (as in "antibiotic"); a stimulant or depressant; to enslave the heart. (Also see Wine)

Reference:Pr 20:1; 31:6-7; Isa 28:1; Hos 4:11; Mt 27:34; Mk 15:23; 1Tim 5:23.

Drunk – *Lack of self-control:* Stubborn; rebellious; fool; to be exposed with shame; under the influence of the Holy Spirit or demonic power; influenced; possessed; controlled; intoxication; impaired faculties; poverty; sorrow; discouragement; self-indulgence; desolation; pride.

Reference:Dt 21:20; 29:19; Pr 20:1; 21:17; 23:21; Isa 28:3; Jer 13:13-14; Hab 2:15-16; Lk 21:34; Acts 2:13-18; 1Cor 5:11; 6:9-10; Eph 5:18; 1Tim 2:2-3.

Dungeon – *Prison:* Captive; confinement; affliction; punishment; bondage to sin; satan; hell; pit; hole. (Also see Basement, Bird Cage, and Prison)

Reference:Lev 24:12; Num 15:34; 1Ki 22:27; Ps 142:7; Isa 42:7; 61:1; Jer 32:2; 37:15-16; Mt 5:25; Rev 20:7.

Dust – *Humiliation:* Grief; mourning; degradation; humble submission; grave; death; low condition; contempt; rejection; dejection; man's body; man's mortality; descendants; judgment; act of cursing.

Reference:Gen 3:19; 13:16; Dt 28:24; Josh 7:6; 1Sam 2:8; 2Sam 16:13; Job 2:12; 7:21; Ps 22:15; 72:9; Isa 26:19; 47:1; Lam 3:29; Mt 10:14; Acts 13:51; 22:23; 1Cor 15:47-49; Rev 18:19.

E

Eagle – *Great and powerful:* Wisdom and revelation, spiritual renewal; leader; prophet (true or false); God's strong and loving care of His people; swiftness; soar high; exchange of strength; proud and haughty spirit (Ob 4); America.

Reference:Ex 19:4; Dt 28:49; Job 9:26; Ps 103:5; Pr 23:5; 30:19; Isa 40:31; Jer 49:16; Lk 17:37; Eph 1:17-18; Rev 12:14.

Ears – *Hearing:* Understanding; to pay careful attention to; channel to receiving faith; to perceive.

Reference:Gen 35:4; Dt 15:17; Ps 18:6; 78:1; 115:6; 135:17; Pr 2:2; Mt 13:9,15-16,43; Rom 10:17; 11:8.

    Deaf ears (stopped up ears) – *Unwilling to hear:* Deaf; dulled; disobedient; to turn from truth.

    Reference:Ps 58:4; Isa 48:8; 64:4; Jer 7:23-24; Mt 13:15; Acts 7:57; 2Tim 4:3-4.

East – *Rising:* Beginning; the sun-rising; place of God's glory; before; anticipate; the front; first; birth; false religion (Eastern religion).

Reference:Gen 3:24; 11:2; 41:23,27; Ex 10:13; Josh 11:3; Ps 103:12; Zech 8:7; Mt 2:2,9; 24:27; Rev 7:2.

Earthquake – *Shaking:* Upheaval; crisis; to quake; change; trial; God's judgment; the wrath of God; trauma; disaster; to agitate; unrest; disturbance.

Reference:Isa 29:6; Ezek 38:19; Mt 27:54; Act 16:26.

Egg – *Potential:* To break out; new idea; new thought; plan; to gather.

Reference:Isa 10:14; Lk 11:12; 1Tim 4:15.

Elephant – *Thick-skinned:* Invincible; unconquerable; proven against attack; not easily offended; of great value (ivory); greatness; old memories.

Reference:Ex 15:7; 1Ki 10:22; 2Chr 9:21; Isa 63:1.

> **White elephant** – *Rejected:* Not wanted; to throw out; to give away; worthless.

> **Baby elephant** – *Potential for greatness:* Beginning of something big; great possibilities, likelihood of becoming successful.

> **Elephant ears** – *Good listener:* Sensitive hearing.

> Reference:Isa 59:1.

Elevator – *Changing position:* Rising up or down in position; from one level to another; up or down motion; elevated; rising into the spirit realm; self-exaltation. (Also see Attic, Stairs/upstairs, Up/Upstairs, and Upper room)

Reference:Gen 28:12; 2Ki 19:22; Ps 73:8; Rev 4:1.

> **Going down** – *Demotion:* Descend; backsliding; lower rank or grade; reduce; trial; dying.

> Reference:Gen 28:12; Ex 17:11-12; Ps 22:29; Pr 14:14; Isa 38:18-19; Jer 3:6-22.

> **Top floor** – *Lofty:* Mind; lid; covering; roof; rank; excel; superior; dignity; social position; high place; high places; above; haughty.

Reference:1Ki 17:19; 2Ki 4:11; 19:22; Job 5:11; 16:19; Ps 73:8; Pr 30:13; Isa 2:11-12; Acts 9:39; 20:8.

Ground floor – *Beginning:* Groundwork; belief; foundation; justification; knowledge; logos.

Reference:Gen 1:1; Ps 111:10; Pr 1:7; Jn 1:1-2; Col 1:18; 1Jn 1:1; Rev 1:8; 3:14.

Emerald – *Glory of God:* Royalty; eternity; prosperity.

Reference:Ezek 28:13; Rev 4:3; 21:19.

Employee – *Servant:* Commissioned by Christ; self; actual employee; subject to examination.

Reference:Gen 3:17-19; Mt 9:37; Lk 12:43-47; Jn 4:38; 1Cor 3:9; Gal 6:4; Col 4:1.

Employer – *Authority:* Jesus Christ; pastor; self; control; superior; power user; the person in charge; one who gives orders; satan; actual employer.

Reference:Col 4:1; 1Tim 6:2.

Enemy – *Adversary:* Those who oppose; satan; the gospel's enemy; a rival; opponent; oppressor; one who sows evil; the accuser of the brethren; deceiver; wickedness; Christians are commanded to love them; death.

Reference:1Sam 1:6; Est 7:6; Ps 139:20-24; Pr 24:17; Mt 5:43-44; 13:25-39; Rom 12:20-21; 1Cor 15:25-26; 16:9; 1Pet 5:8-9; Rev 12:10; 20:10.

Evening Gown – *Formal event:* A formal manner; ceremonious; formal in character; pomp and circumstance; fancy.

Reference:Mt 22:11-12.

Eyes – *Sight:* The ability to see; revealed knowledge; understanding; enlightenment; insight; sight; foresight; agreement (as in "eye to eye"); lamp (light or darkness); worldliness; lust; desires (good or evil).

Reference:Num 24:2-4; Ps 19:8; 101:3-6; Pr 23:5; 27:20; Isa 52:8; Mt 6:22-23; Eph 1:18; 2Pet 2:14; 1Jn 2:16.

Eyes open – *Insight received:* Revelation acquired; to see; to know and understand.

Reference:Gen 3:7; Num 22:31; 2Ki 6:17-18; Ps 119:18; Isa 35:5-6; Lk 24:31.

Eyes closed – *Insight withheld:* Blindness; spiritual blindness; deception; confusion.

Reference:Gen 19:11; 21:19; Lk 24:16.

F

Face – *Heart:* Expression; character; the face of someone in a mirror may be reflecting his or your own heart (Pr 27:19); confidence; boldness; to confront; front (as in "face the music"); outward appearance; surface; worship (as in "falling on our face"); mourning (as in "covering of"); disapproval (as in "hiding of"); determination (as in "setting your face"); rejection (as in "turning away").

Reference:Gen 17:3; Dt 31:17-18; 2Sam 19:4; 2Ki 9:30; 12:17; 2Chr 30:9; Pr 21:29; 27:19; Jer 13:26; Hos 7:2; 1Cor 13:12; 14:25; 2Cor 3:18; Jam 1:23.

God's face – *His presence:* His manifest glory; brightness (as in "shine on"); favor; anger; justice; severity; fear; reverence.

Reference:Gen 32:30; Ex 3:6; 33:20; Num 6:25; Dt 31:17-18; Ps 67:1; Dan 9:17; 1Pet 3:12; Rev 6:16.

Factory – *Production:* Work; works; serve; labor; to bear fruit; to make; to construct; efficient; to accomplish; to prepare; to create; to make ready; the act or process; progress; operate in unison; action; method of procedure; occupation; system; strategy; the kingdom of God; the church.

Reference:Gen 1:1,7,11; 5:29; 6:14; Ex 25:8; 26:1; 31:3-4; 1Chr 28:10; Ps 90:17; Pr 31:13; Ezek 17:8.

Falcon: (See Hawk)

Falling – *To descend from a high position to a lower position:* To drop from position; to be lowered; to suddenly or involuntarily drop; demotion; to fall in rank, position or status; stumble; stray; to become captured; to fall into the hands of the enemy; ruin; defeat; failure; immorality; unsupported; to drop in value; to fall short of God's glory; to fall in love; to fall prostrate and worship

God; to stumble; backslide; to fall into temptation; to fall short; out of control; lack of support; to go down; decline; the season after summer; social or spiritual worsening; judgment of sin and pride; apostasy (falling away from God's truth).

Reference:Gen 3:6; Ps 17:5; 56:13; 116:8; Jer 5:6; Mt 26:39; Lk 8:47; Rom 3:23; 1Cor 14:25; 2Thes 2:3-4; 2Pet 1:10; Jude 24.

Family – *Spiritual Family:* Relatives; common ancestry; common characteristics; natural family; heritage; inheritance; live in unity; descendant; kinship; relationship.

Reference:Gen 18:19; Josh 24:15; Gal 4:5; 6:10; Eph 2:19; 6:4; 1Tim 5:1.

Farm – *Field of Labor:* Sowing seed; the harvest; harvesting; kingdom of God; the church; ministry; husbandman; vine-dresser; work; works; where you labor; cultivation of a field; service; physical efforts; manual labor. (Also see Country)

Reference:Gen 2:15; 26:12-14; 37:7; Dt 11:10; Ps 103:15; Isa 28:24; 61:5; Jer 14:4; 31:24; 51:23; Amos 5:16; 9:13; Joel 1:10-11; Mic 4:10; Mt 9:37-38; 13:38-39; 20:1; 22:1-5; Jn 4:35; 2Cor 9:10; 2Tim 2:6; Jas 5:7.

Farmer – *Laborer:* Tiller of the soil; pastor; Christ; ministry workers; harvesters; the church.

Reference:Gen 4:12; Pr 12:11; 24:30-34; Eccl 1:3; Mk 4:14; Jn 15:1-8; 2Cor 9:10.

Father – *God:* Authority; superior; originator; counselor; creator; source; natural father; training; instructing; source; disciplining; nourishment; supplier; tradition; inheritance.

Reference:Gen 28:13; 37:4; 45:8; Dt 21:18-21; 2Ki 2:12; Job 38:28; Pr 1:8; Isa 1:2; Mt 7:8-11; 23:9; 1Thess 2:11; Jas 1:17.

Feet – *Walk:* Way; path; course of walking; manner of living; conduct; behavior; discipleship (as in "to sit at the feet of"); teachable; subjection; submission; stability; preparation; humility and worship (as in "to fall at the feet"); dance; conquest (as in "to put under the feet"); hospitality (as in "to wash the feet of"); great love (as in "to kiss the feet of"); rejection (as in "shake off the dust of your feet"); preaching the gospel.

Reference:Josh 10:24; 1Sam 25:24,41; Ps 40:2; Pr 1:15-16; 4:26-27; Isa 14:25; Mt 10:14; Lk 7:38; 7:44-46; 10:39; Jn 13:4-15; Acts 22:3; Rom 10:15; Eph 6:15.

Barefoot – *Unprepared:* Reverence; distress; shame; embarrassment; mourning; too fast; not protected.

Reference:Ex 3:5; 2Sam 15:30; Isa 20:1-4; Mic 1:8; Lk 15:22.

Big Toe – *Headship:* To walk with God; to have God's guidance in our walk; for God to direct our path; to walk in God's ways; to consecrate oneself.

Reference:Ex 29:20; Lev 8:23-24; 14:14,17,25,28; Jdg 1:6.

Fence – *Barrier:* Boundary; God's protection or the removal of God's protection; hindrance; obstacle; to divide; separate; wall; hedge; religious traditions; doctrines; enclosed; indecision; to keep in or out; defense; offense; debate; slothfulness. (Also see Walls)

Reference:Job 1:10; 19:8; Ps 62:3; 80:12; Pr 15:19; Eccl 10:8; SS 4:12; Isa 5:5; Ezek 22:30; Hos 2:6; Mt 21:33; Lk 14:23.

Field – *Harvest of souls:* World; one's entire inheritance; cultivated land; potential harvest; region or territory of people.

Reference:Lev 27:16-24; Ruth 4:5; Pr 24:30-34; Jer 32:9; Joel 1:10-12; Mt 13:38-39; 1Cor 3:9.

Finger – *Power and authority of God:* Direction; measurement.

Reference:Ex 8:19; Dt 9:10; Ps 8:3; Pr 6:13; Lk 11:20.

Pointing finger – *Accusation:* to point blame.

Fire – *Purifying:* Holy Spirit; God's presence and power; to refine; to consume; testing; judgment; anger; jealousy; strong emotion; God's wrath against rebellion; eternal damnation.

Reference:Gen 15:17-18; Ex 32:10-11; Dt 4:24; Ps 79:5; Amos 5:6; Mal 3:2; Mt 3:10-12; Lk 24:32; Acts 2:3; Heb 12:29; Rev 20:9-10.

Fire Department or Police Department – *Service:* Save; rescue; to make safe; to deliver; salvation; help; defend; spiritual warfare, power; authority (God's or man's); those in authority (governments, employers, parents, pastors, elders, etc).

Reference:Dt 28:31; 1Sam 14:45; Ps 35:17; Pr 29:2; Isa 30:15; 40; Dan 6:27; Hos 5:14; Acts 23:27; Rom 13:1-7; Eph 6:11-12; Heb 13:7,17.

Fish – *Soul of man:* Man; clean or unclean; men in the sea of life; spirit; character of a person; church; Jesus Christ; Holy Spirit.

Reference:Ezek 47:9-10; Mt 4:18-19; 13:47-48; Mk 1:17; Luke 11:11; 1Cor 15:39.

Flea – *Annoying:* Nuisance; irritant; insignificant. (Also Tick).

Reference:1Sam 24:14; 26:20.

Lice – *Filthy:* Unclean; pest. (Also Gnat).

Reference:Ex 8:16-18; Ps 105:31.

Flies – *Corruption:* Devour; decay; destroy; demon; annoying; nuisance; plague.

Reference:Ex 8:21-31; Ps 78:45; 105:31; Eccl 10:1.

Maggot – *Corruption:* Filthiness of the flesh; devourer; decay.

Reference:Job 13:28; Ps 22:6; Pr 10:7.

Flying: (See **Airplane: Flying or soaring**).

Flint – *Hardness:* Sharpness; a fixed course; hardheaded; hardhearted. (Also see Diamond)

Reference:Josh 5:2-3; Job 28:9; Ps 114:8; Isa 5:28; 50:7; Ezek 3:9; Zech 7:12.

Flood – *Judgment (good or bad):* Overwhelming circumstances; great trouble; great destruction; testing; persecution; to fill to overflowing; to pour forth; deluge; drown; overflow; run over; being swept away (good or bad).

Reference:Gen 6:13,17; Job 22:16; Ps 32:6; 90:5; Isa 54:9; Dan 9:26; Mt 7:25-27; 24:38-39; Heb 11:7; Rev 12:15-16.

Flowers – *Fragrance of God:* Temporary; gifts; anointing; love; shortness of life; beauty; fading; glory of man; mankind; the season of spring.

Reference:Job 14:2; Ps 103:15; SS 2:12; Isa 40:7-8; Mt 6:28-29; Jam 1:10-11.

Forehead – *To shine:* Devotion to God; stubborn (as in "of a hard forehead"); mind; peace of mind; memory; courage; thoughts;

reason, imagination; Christ's true servants; stronger power; shamelessness.

Reference:Ex 28:38; Ezek 3:7-9; 9:4-6; Rev 7:3; 9:4; 13:16; 17:5.

Food – *Nourishment:* Spiritual food; source of energy; to sustain; supply; sustenance; provision; provision from God; to satisfy; the wisdom of the Word; to feed on the Word of God.

Reference:Ps 78:18,25; 111:5; 136:25; 145:15; 146:7; Pr 6:8; Mal 3:10; Mt 14:15-21; 25:35-46; Jn 6:55-58; Act 9:19; Rom 14:15-23; 1Cor 3:2; 8:13; 10:3; Heb 5:12-14; Jas 2:15-16;

Foreigner – *Outsider:* Alien; not of God; foreign God; belonging to another nation; representative of another nation; stranger; gentile; demonic; not of this world. (Also see Indian)

Reference:Ex 12:43, 48-49; Dt 14:21; 23:20; Josh 24:20; 1Ki 11:1; Ps 144:7,11; Isa 56:3-7; Jer 5:19; Acts 11:3; 1Cor 14:11; Eph 2:19.

Forest – *World:* Unfruitfulness; nations; kingdom; army; sin; darkness; wilderness; kingdom of darkness; corruption; fear; confusion. (Also Jungle)

Reference:Ps 104:20; 107:4-5; Isa 10:17-19,34; 29:17; 32:15,19; Jer 21:14; 26:18; Hos 2:12; Jam 3:5.

Lost in the forest – *Confusion:* No direction; helpless; to wander; separated from God; blinded by satan; to be led astray.

Reference:Ps 27:13; 119:176; Jer 50:6; Mt 10:6; 15:24; Lk 15:4-6,24,32; 2Cor 4:3-4.

Foundation – *Established:* Christ; stable or unstable; supported or unsupported; permanent; base; righteousness and justice; groundwork; rest; justification; fundamentals; essentials; firm or shifting. (Also see Basement)

Reference:Ps 11:3; 87:1; 89:14; 102:25; Isa 28:16; Mt 16:18; Lk 6:48; 14:29; 1Cor 3:10-11; Eph 2:20; Heb 6:1-2.

Fountain – *Refreshing:* The source of life.

Fox – *Deception:* Sly; cunning; subtle; hidden sin; false prophet; enemy; deceivers; evil men; destructive; crafty; such blood of lambs.

Reference:SS 2:15; Ezek 13:1-4,6; Neh 4:3; Mt 8:20; Lk 9:58; 13:32.

Friend – *Self:* Representative of another friend; may represent actual friend; Jesus; trustworthy or untrustworthy; faithful; valuable; companion; comrade; love; sacrifice.

Reference:Gen 38:12; 1Sam 20:17; Ps 41:9; Pr 17:17-18; 27:6, 9-10; Jn 3:29; 15:13.

Frog – *Spirit or demon:* Witchcraft; lust; sexual lust; curse; plague; evil spirit; unclean; renewal; life; happiness; counterfeit.

Reference:Ex 8:1-15; Ps 78:45; 105:30; Rev 16:13.

Front – *Present or future:* Prophetic; current; immediate; revealed; manifest; exposed; gate or entrance; public; open to the world. (Also see Porch)

Reference: Gen 6:11; Joel 2:17; Acts 10:17; 12:14; 14:13; Rev 1:19.

Fruit – *Righteousness:* Product of life; Christian converts; repentance; Christ; rewards; evidence; efforts; offspring; children.

Reference:Ps 92:14; 132:11; Mal 3:11; Mt 3:8-10; 7:16-19; Jn 4:36; 15:2-8; Gal 5:22-23; Phil 1:11,22; 2Pet 1:5-11.

Almond – *Awakening:* Waker (because of the early blossoming of the almond tree); watching; to hasten (as in God's haste in fulfilling His promises); dependability; rejuvenation; fruitfulness.

Reference:Ex 25:33-34; Num 17:8; Jer 1:11-12.

Apple – *Value:* God's care and protection; the apple of God's eye.

Reference:Dt 32:10; Ps 17:8; Pr 7:2; Zech 2:8.

Fig – *Peace and prosperity:* Divine favor; productiveness; security and hope; desolation; barren religion.

Reference:Gen 3:7; 1Ki 4:25; Jer 8:13; 24:1-10; Mt 21:19; Lk 13:6-9.

Funeral – *A burial ceremony:* Dead to sin but alive to God; buried with Him in baptism and raised with Him through faith in His resurrection; mourning; to lay at rest or to put at rest.

Reference:Gen 37:34; 50:25; Rom 6:4-14; 1Cor 15:4; Col 2:12-13.

G

Garden – *Fruitfulness:* Righteousness; prosperity; work or labor; field of labor; fruit of one's labor; offering; gifts; anointing; growth; intimacy; love; desolation.

Reference:Gen 3:1-3; Ps 65:10; Isa 10:18; 51:3; 58:11; 61:11; Jer 2:21; Joel 2:3; Amos 4:9; Lk 13:19; Php 1:22.

Gate or Gateway – *Point or place of access:* Opening; entrance; door; way; power and authority; port; portal; protection; narrow and difficult is the gate. (Also see Door, Portal, or Window)

Reference:2Sam 18:24,33; Ps 118:19-20; Pr 26:14; Jer 17:19-20; Mt 6:6; 7:13-14; 16:18-19; 25:10; Lk 11:5-10; Rev 21:25.

Gatekeeper – *Watchman:* Intercessor; to keep watch; to oversee what goes in and what goes out; porter; guard. (Also see Guardian)

Reference:2Sam 18:26-27; 2Chr 35:15; Neh 12:25; Ps 84:10; 127:1; 141:3; Isa 52:8; 59:16; Jer 51:12; Ezek 33:6-7; Mk 13:33-34; Jn 10:3; 18:16-17.

Ghost – *Holy Spirit:* Angel; one's spirit or soul; demon; a false image.

Reference:Gen 25:8; Ps 51:11-12; Jer 15:9; Dan 4:8-9; Mt 1:18-20; 3:11; 12:32; Mk 6:49; Lk 4:1; 7:21; 8:2; Jn 3:6-8; 6:63; 7:39; Acts 1:5; 19:11-16.

Giant – *Strongman:* Strength; power; to control by force; tyrant; stronghold; trouble; spiritual warfare; obstacle to be overcome; challenge; opposition; obstacle; one's own carnal nature; trouble.

Reference:Gen 6:4-6; Num 13:32-33; 1Sam 17:4,23-54; Ps 19:5; Nah 1:7; Mt 12:29; Mk 3:27; Lk 11:21; Acts 3:16.

Gifts – *Something freely given:* Cannot be bought; spiritual endowments or talents given by the Holy Spirit for the works of the ministry, for the purpose of drawing all men to Himself; offering; donation; contribution; free gift; counterfeited by satan.

Reference:Pr 19:6; Lk 11:13; Acts 8:18-20; Rom 1:11; 1Cor 12; 2Cor 11:13-15; Phil 4:19; 1Tim 6:17; Jam 1:17-18; 4:6.

Glass – *Transparent:* Clear; clear or poor reflection (as in a mirror); vision (as in "glass lenses"); to see; revelation; Christ's glory; God's nature; container or vessel; holiness and purity (as in the Sea of Glass); fragile; breakable. (Also see Crystal)

Reference:Eccl 12:6; Isa 8:9; Dan 2:42; 1Cor 13:12; 2Cor 3:18; Jas 1:23; Rev 4:6; 15:2; 21:18-21.

Goat – *Christ:* Great leader; our sin offering; sinner; the righteous and the wicked; unbelief; unyielding; argumentative; wicked; negative; scapegoat; stubborn; those destined for eternal punishment. (Also see **Cattle** and **Sheep**)

Reference:Ex 12:5; Lev 16:10,15; 22:19; Jer 50:8; Ezek 34:17; Mt 25:32-46.

Gold – *Refined:* Purification; refined saints; redeemed; doctrine of Christ; kingship; glory; separate; treasure; wisdom; knowledge; holiness; precious; durable; glory of God; value; wealth; offerings; beauty; idolatry; self-glorification; idolatry.

Reference:Ex 12:35; 32:31; 35:22; 1Ki 6:20-22; 7:48-50; 10:21; Job 23:10; 28:15; Ps 19:10; 21:3; 119:127; Pr 8:19; SS 5:11; Isa 13:12; 41:7; 44:12-13; Lam 4:1-2; Zech 9:3; Col 2:3; 2Tim 2:20; Jas 2:2-4; 1Pet 1:7; Rev 3:18.

Governor – *Ruler:* Authority; Christ; pastor; ministry leader; provincial leader; the person in control; lawgiver; one who carries out justice; officer of high rank; one who governs the people.

Reference: Gen 42:6; 2Chro 23:20; Ezra 6:6-8; 8:36; Neh 8:9; Mt 27:2-27; Acts 23:24-35.

Grandchild – *Heritage:* Heir; offspring; descendant; oneself; crown; legacy; spiritual inheritance; inheritance; inherited blessing or iniquity; actual grandchild.

Reference: Gen 15:13-18; Ex 34:7; Dt 5:8-10; Job 18:19; Ps 127:3; Pr 17:6; Isa 14:22; 1Tim 5:4.

Grandmother (or Grandfather) - *Spiritual inheritance:* Past; inherited blessings or iniquity; elder; wisdom; legacy; heritage; spiritual inheritance; old; actual grandmother or grandfather.

Reference: Gen 17:7-8; Ex 6:8; 1Ki 15:9-13; 1Tim 1:3-5.

Grass – *Flesh:* Frailty of the flesh; temporary; shortness of life.

Reference: Ps 90:5-6; 92:7; Isa 15:6; Zech 10:1; 1Pet 1:24.

Grasshopper – *Inferior:* Small; insignificant; plague; burden; destroyer; enemies; evil spirit. (Also see **Butterfly/Caterpillar** and **Locust**)

Reference: Num 13:33; Jdg 6:5; 7:12; 2Chr 6:28-30; Isa 40:22; 46:23; Joel 1:4; Amos 7:1; Nah 3:17.

Gray – *Not clear:* Not definite; vague; wishy-washy (as in "riding the fence"); indecisive; obscure; indistinct; fuzzy; wanderer; undecided; the splendor of a man (gray hair); false doctrine; deception; deceived; hazy; depression; sorrow.

Reference: Gen 42:38; 44:29-31; Pr 20:29; Isa 46:4; Hos 7:9.

Green – *Life:* Freshness; vigor; prosperity; flourishing; growth; hope; ripeness; good fruit; yielding fruit; putting forth; sprouting; renewal; beauty; mortality; carnality; flesh; young; new; renewal; to flourish; envy; resentment; pride. (Also see Grass and Tree)

Reference:Ex 10:15; Lev 2:14; Job 8:11-18; 15:32; Ps 23:2; 37:2,35; 52:8; 92:10-15; SS 1:16; 2:13; Jer 11:16; 17:8; Lk 23:31; 1Pet 2:24.

Guardian – *Watchman:* Protector; helper; steward; safeguard against harm; one who watches over something or someone; guardian angel. (Also see **Gate/Gatekeeper**)

Reference:Gen 24:7; Num 11:12; Est 2:7; Ps 91:11; Mt 18:10; Acts 19:35; Gal 4:1-2; 2Tim 1:12.

Guerilla – *Intimidation:* Harassment; frighten; to compel or deter by or as if by threats; warfare; war; terrorize; strife; irregular warfare by independent bands; harassment; sabotage; independent; to cause confusion; Africa.

Reference:Lk 3:14; 1Cor 14:33; Gal 1:6-7; 5:7-15; Php 2:3; Jam 3:16.

Guide – *Leader:* God; Holy Spirit; to go before; advise; to conduct; to protect; to direct; lead; to show the way; to be the head of a family; integrity of the upright; instructor or teacher; instigator.

Reference:Ps 31:3; 32:8; 48:14; 73:24; 112:5; Pr 11:3; 23:19; Isa 49:10; 58:11; Jer 3:4; Lk 1:79; Jn 16:13; Acts 1:16; Rom 2:19.

H

Hail – *Judgment:* Destruction; ruin; penalty; plague; punishment. (Also see Ice)

Reference:Ex 9:18-29; 33-34; Ps 78:47-48; 105:32; 147:17; Isa 28:2, 17; Ezek 38:22; Hag 2:17.

Hair – *Covering:* Glory; covenant (Nazarite); outward adorning; strength.

Reference:Num 6:5; Jdg 16:17-22; 1Cor 11:15-16; 1Tim 2:9; 1Pet 3:3.

Baldness – *No covering:* Mourning; lamentation.

Reference:Lev 21:5; Dt 14:1; 2Ki 2:23; Ezek 27:31; Mic 1:16.

Haircut – *Cutting off wisdom or strength:* Loss of strength or power; cutting off the anointing; to reshape understanding; cutting away the old; to trim edges; to break covenant (as in the Nazarite vow); a vow; to remove one's covering.

Reference:Num 6:1-8; Dt 14:1; Jdg 16:17:22; Mic 1:16; Acts 18:18; 1Cor 11:15-16.

Gray hair – *Wisdom:* Glory; age; weakness.

Reference:1Sam 12:2; Job 15:10; Pr 16:31; 20:29; Hos 7:9.

Long hair – *Glory:* Covering; strength.

Reference:Jdg 16:17; 1Cor 11:15.

White hair – *Honor:* Authority; respect; age; wisdom; approaching decay.

Reference:1Sam 12:2; Pr 16:31; Dan 7:9; Hos 7:9; Rev 1:14.

Hall or Hallway – *Place of transition or decision:* An entrance (as in an entry hallway); passageway; place of waiting; place of judgment (hall of judgment); the place for the throne of judgment; place of assembly (as in "wedding hall" or "banquet hall").

Reference:1Sam 9:22; 1Ki 7:7; Dan 5:10; Mt 22:10; 27:27; Mk 15:16; Jn 18:28,33; Acts 23:35.

Hammer – *The Word of God:* Breaker; to pound; striking action; to beat; to drive; repeated blows; tool for creative or destructive means; a false witness.

Reference:Jdg 4:21; 5:26; Pr 25:18; Isa 41:7; Jer 23:29.

Hands – *Works:* Deeds; human action (good or evil); labor; service; ministry; power and strength; relationship; worship; covenant; agreement; possession; to inflict punishment; judgment; idolatry.

Reference:Ex 15:6; 2Ki 3:11; 10:15; Job 17:3; Ps 17:7; 28:4; 81:14; 115:4; 128:2; Pr 14:1; Jer 6:9; Ezek 38:12.

Clapping hands – *Joy:* Worship; triumph; extreme anger.

Reference:Num 24:10; 2Ki 11:12; Ps 47:1; 98:8; Isa 55:12; Ezek 21:14,17.

Closed hand – *Lack:* Stinginess; not generous, giving or spending as little as possible; unwilling to spend or share with those in need, miser.

Reference:Dt 15:7; Pr 23:6; Isa 32:5; Mal 1:10.

Left hand – *Judgment:* North; riches and honor.

Reference:Job 23:9; Pr 3:16; SS 2:6; Ezek 39:3; Zech 12:6; Mt 6:3; 25:41; 2Cor 6:4-10.

Open hand – *Liberality:* Generosity; bounty.

Reference:Dt 15:8; Ps 104:28; Pr 11:25; 22:9; Isa 32:8; 58:7; Acts 10:2; 2Cor 9:5; Heb 13:16.

Raised hands – *Worship:* Prayer (clasped together); surrender; oath, covenant; length of days.

Reference:Gen 14:22; Job 11:13; Pr 3:16; Dan 12:7; Zech 12:6; 1Tim 2:8.

Right hand – *Power and strength:* Support; protection; place of honor and power; blessing; the Lord's help; south.

Reference:Ex 15:6; 1Ki 2:19; Ps 16:8; 17:7; 109:31; 110:5; SS 2:6; Isa 41:13; Ezek 39:3; Mt 6:3; 25:33; Mk 14:62; 2Cor 6:4-10.

Shaking hands – *Agreement:* Covenant; promise; pledge.

Reference:2Ki 23:3; Neh 9:38; Pr 17:18; 22:26; Isa 36:8; Ezek 18:7,12,16; 33:15.

Washing hands – *Innocence:* Cleansing.

Reference:Lev 15:11; Dt 21:6-7; Ps 26:6; 73:13; Mt 15:2; 27:24; Mk 7:3.

Harvest – *To gather:* Reward of efforts; a mature crop; reap; glean; fruits of labor; measure of fruitfulness; gospel opportunities; ripe; righteous or wicked; to separate; end of the age.

Reference:Gen 8:22; Pr 10:5; 20:4; Isa 9:3; 17:11; Joel 1:11; 3:13; Amos 4:7; Mt 9:37-38; 13:39; 2Cor 9:6; Rev 14:15.

Hawk – *Predator:* Evil spirit; war or warfare; unclean; one who stalks; false prophets. (Also see **Falcon**)

Reference:Lev 11:13-16; Dt 14:15; Job 39:26; Isa 34:15.

Hay: (See Crops/Hay and Grass)

Head – *Authority:* God; Christ; man; husband; position; protection; mind; knowledge; understanding; pride.

Reference:Ex 29:6-7; Ps 27:6; 68:21; Ps 83:2; 140:7; Eccl 2:14; 1Cor 11:3-13; Eph 1:22; Col 1:18; 2:10,19.

Headless – *Without authority:* Without power; without guidance or direction; foolish; lack of leadership; open to the works of the enemy; as in "sheep without a shepherd" or "a ship without its captain."

Reference:Num 27:17; 1Sam 31:9-10; 1Ki 22:17; 1Chr 10:9-10; 2Chr 18:16; Mt 9:36; Mk 6:34; 1Pet 2:25.

Uncovered head – *No cover or protection:* No spiritual covering; no insurance or security; bare; naked; unclean; exposed; revealed.

Reference:Lev 14:8-9; Num 6:18-19; Job 1:20; Isa 7:20; Ezek 44:20; Hos 7:1; 1Cor 11:5-13.

Heart – *Condition of man:* Innermost being; life; emotions; motivations; feelings and affections; desires; center for thought (good and evil); the seat of love; hatred; the center of the moral life and moral conditions; dwelling place of Christ and the Holy Spirit.

Reference:Lev 19:17; Dt 29:4; Ps 40:8-12; 73:26; Pr 14:10; Isa 65:14; Mt 12:34-35; Lk 8:15; Rom 6:17; 1Cor 7:37; 2Cor 1:22; Eph 3:13-17; 1Tim 1:5.

Heel – *Victory:* The overcoming of an enemy; overwhelm; suppress.

Reference:Gen 3:15; 25:26; 49:17; Job 18:5-9; Ps 41:9; Jn 13:18; Rom 16:20.

Helicopter – *Versatile:* Ministry or person; individual; church; vertically rising; to go straight up in the Spirit; maneuverability; evasive movement; conspire; plot.

Helmet: (See Armor/Helmet of Salvation)

Hill – *Smaller trials:* Something that is elevated; lifted up; overcoming obstacles; place of worship; elevation; loftiness.

Reference:Josh 5:3; Ps 3:4; 99:9; Pr 8:2; Isa 40:4; Jer 2:20; Ezek 34:6; Mt 5:14; Lk 3:5; 23:30.

Homosexuality – *Uncleanness:* Unnatural passion or desire; perversion; lusts of the heart; forbidden relationship; fornication.

Reference:Lev 18:22-23; 20:13; 1Ki 15:12; Rom 1:24-27; 1Cor 6:9-10; 1Tim 1:10; Rev 17:5.

Hornet: (See **Bees**).

Horse – *Strength:* Power; swift; God's protection; burden bearer; travel; spiritual support; power of the flesh (as in "works of the flesh"); God's Spirit working through man; war; warfare; victory; work; sending messages; idolatry.

Reference:Ex 14:9; Dt 17:16; 2Ki 2:11; 23:11; Neh 7:68; Est 8:10; Job 39:18-19; Ps 32:9, Jer 5:8, 8:6; Zech 10:3; Rev 19:19.

Donkey (mule) – *Stubborn:* Self-willed; unyielding; obstinate; stupid; sturdy; burden-bearer; patient; sign of kingship;

obnoxious; working; peaceful mission; surefooted. (Also see **Ass, Colt,** or **Mule**)

Reference:Num 22:25-27; 1Ki 1:33; Pr 26:3; Isa 30:24; 32:20; Mt 21:5-7; 2Pet 2:16.

Braying – *Bragging:* Boastful; complain (as in "to toot one's own horn).

Reference:Job 6:5, 30:7.

Horse's rider – *Striving:* Work; endurance; anxious; conqueror; confidence.

Reference:Ex 15:1,21; 2Ki 4:24; Job 39:18; Jer 51:21; Zech 12:4; Rev 6:2,8.

Black horse – *Famine:* Pestilence; lack; shortage; inadequate supply; bad times.

Reference:Amos 8:11; Rev 6:5.

Red horse – *War:* Persecution; opposition; danger.

Reference:Zech 1:8; Jn 16:2; Rev 6:4.

White horse – *Purity and strength:* Indestructible; invincible; victory; power; Jesus Christ.

Reference:Zech 1:8; Rev 6:2; 19:11-19.

Kicking/lifting heel – *Objection:* Disapproval; rebellion; opposition; persecution; aim; purpose.

Reference:1Sam 2:29; 2Sam 16:13; Ps 41:9; Jn 13:18; Acts 9:5; 26:14.

Quarter horse – *Strength:* Endurance; fast; speed; success.

Reference:Rev 6:2.

Hospital – *Healing:* Care; mercy; cure; helps; comforts and soothes; sick or wounded; the church.

Reference:Ex 15:26; Ps 103:3; 109:22; 147:3; Isa 30:26; 53:5; Jer 8:22; 17:14; 30:17; Mt 4:24; 9:12-13; Mk 5:25-27; Lk 10:30,33-34.

Hotel – *Hospitality:* Receive; rest; lodge; travel; business travel; guest; provisions.

Reference:Gen 18:1-8; 19:1-3; 24:25, Lev 19:34; Lk 9:12; Acts 10:23; 28:15; Rom 12:13.

House – *Family or individual person:* Descendants; tabernacle or temple; church; home; residence; dwelling; sanctuary; heart (as in "home is where the heart is"); individuality; essential character; roots; security or insecurity; division.

Reference:Gen 7:1; 14:14; 18:19; 19:2; Ex 2:1; 23:19; 34:26; Josh 7:14; Jdg 11:34; 1Sam 20:16; 1Ki 6:1; 1Chr 17:5; Job 17:13; Ps 132:3; Mt 7:24-27; Mk 3:25; Lk 2:4; 11:24; Acts 16:31-32.

New house – *New life:* Change; new ministry; to replace with another; transform; revival; new position or posture; to go from one point to another; change of location.

Reference:Jer 31:31; Ezek 18:31; 2Cor 3:6; 5:1,17; Heb 8:8.

Old house – *Past or previous:* Religious inheritance; inheritance; heritage; established tradition; old ways; old paths; old wineskins.

Reference:Gen 12:1; Jer 6:16; Mt 15:2-3,6; Mk 7:3-13; Gal 1:14; Col 2:8; 1Pet 1:4,18; 3:9.

In good condition – *Righteousness:* Sturdy; earnest; diligent; truth.

Reference:2Tim 1:3; 1Pet 1:4,23; 3:9.

In bad condition – *Sins of the forefathers:* Our sins; need for revival or repair; neglected; untended; ruin; unusable.

Reference:Ps 119; 143:11; Jer 11:10; Rom 1:23; 1Cor 15:53-54.

Hurricane: (See Whirlwind)

Husband – *Authority:* Head, headship; God or Jesus Christ; actual husband; to rule over; satan; covenant; agreement.

Reference:Gen 3:16; Isa 54:5; 1Cor 7; 11:3-7; 2Cor 11:2; Eph 5:25; 1Pet 3:7; Rev 21:2.

I

Ice – *Smooth words:* Breath of God; deceptively ready with answers and explanations; diviner; divination; icy words; slippery; not to be trusted; coldness; hazardous (as in "skating on thin ice"). (Also see **Hail**)

Reference:Gen 31:40; Job 6:16; 37:9-10; 38:29-30; Ps 73:2; 78:47; 147:16-17; Isa 55:10-11; Jer 36:30.

Idol – *Idolatry:* Something being worshipped and looked upon as a god; an image being worshipped as a god; graven image; a false god; something that stands between God and us. (Also see Image)

Reference:Ex 20:4; 34:17; Lev 26:1; Dt 4:28; Ps 24:4; 115:4-7; Isa 2:20; 30:22; 31:7; 48:5; Hos 8:4; 1Cor 8:4-10.

Image – *Likeness:* Imitation of a person or thing; statue; picture; impression; representation of; man made in the image of God; graven image or idol; a false god. (Also see Idol)

Reference:Gen 1:26; Jdg 17:3; Isa 30:22; 48:5; Dan 2:32-33.

Incense – *Offering of prayer and praise to God:* Intercession; worship; an acceptable sacrifice; prayers of the saints; making atonement for.

Reference:Lev 16:12-13; Ps 141:2; Mal 1:11; Mt 2:11; Lk 1:9-11; Eph 5:2; Rev 5:8; 8:3-4.

Indian – *Native:* Native American; belonging to a particular country by birth; natural; relating to a particular country or organization; chief; first; actual person; adversary; fierce. (Also see Foreigner)

Reference:Est 1:1; 8:9.

Insurance – *Assurance:* To cover; to rescue; redeem; redemption; atonement; Christ's salvation; indemnity; to free from the consequences; to remove the obligation; means of protection; financial protection; protection against loss or harm; return for payment; the effect of righteousness.

Reference:Dt 21:8; Job 42:10; Ps 55:18; 78:42; 106:10; 107:2-9; Isa 32:17; 44:22-23; Jer 31:11; Lk 1:68-69; Acts 17:30-31; 1Cor 3:9-14; Gal 3:13-14; Heb 6:12; Rev 5:9.

No Insurance – *Penalty:* To suffer the consequences; to not be covered; no protection; loss or hardship; financial loss.

Reference:Job 11:20; Ezek 23:35; Rom 1:27; 1Cor 3;9-17.

Intercession – *Prayer offered on behalf of others:* To pray for something or someone; to intervene in prayer on behalf of another's circumstances; to petition the Lord in prayer for others; belabored prayer; unselfish prayer; praying according to the will of God; Christ makes intercession for the saints.

Reference:Gen 18:23-33; Ex 8:28; 32:31-33; 1Sam 2:25; 1Chr 29:19; Isa 53:12; Jer 7:16; Lk 22:32; Jn 17; Acts 7:60; Rom 8:26-27,34; 1Tim 2:1; Heb 7:25.

Intestines (bowels) – *The interior self:* Mind, heart and spirit; the control of one's emotions; inmost thoughts or feelings; purposes of the soul; innermost motives; reins.

Reference:Ex 29:13-14,22; Lev 4:9-10; Ps 7:9; 26:2; 49:11; Pr 18:8; 20:27,30; 23:16; Jer 11:20; 12:2; Lk 12:3; Eph 3:16; Rev 2:23.

Intoxication – *Physically and mentally impaired:* Affected by drugs; drunkenness; to become uncovered; foolishness; to be led astray; lusts of the flesh; to surrender your will to the will of another force; sorrow.

Reference:Gen 9:21; 19:32-35; Pr 20:1; Isa 5:11-13,22; Jer 51:57; Ezek 23:33; Lk 21:34; Rom 13:13; 14:21; Gal 5:21.

Iron – *Strength:* Endurance; firm; unyielding; an obstinate (stiff-necked) people; offensive weaponry; yoke; affliction; barrenness; stubbornness; slavery; insensibility.

Reference:Ex 32:9; 33:3,5; Dt 4:20; 28:23,48; 33:25; 1Sam 17:5-7; Isa 48:4; Jer 1:18; 28:13-14; Dan 2:33-45; 7:7,19; Mic 4:13; 1Tim 4:2.

Ironing – *Correction:* To smooth out the wrinkles in one's character; change; sanctification; teaching; discipline from God; to press upon; to be pressed; to be without spot or wrinkle.

Reference:Eph 5:27.

J

Jackal (or Fox) – *Evil scavenger:* satan; smelly beast of the wilderness; desolate habitation; linked with the dragon, fox and wolf; to yap or howl.

Reference:Jdg 15:4-5; Ps 44:19; 63:10; Isa 13:21-22; 34:13-14; Jer 9:11; 10:22; 14:6; Lam 4:3; 5:18; Ezek 13:4; Mal 1:3.

Jasper – *Pure:* Clean; reflector of light and color; heavenly vision; the twelfth stone of the breastplate of judgment (ephod).

Reference:Ex 28:20; 39:13; Ezek 29:13; Rev 4:3; 21:11,18-19.

Jeans – *Durable:* Able to withstand the test; tough; rugged; casual.

Reference:Eccl 4:12.

Jewels – *Wealth:* Tokens of love; tokens of repentance; those who fear the Lord; treasures; worldliness.

Reference:Gen 35:4; Pr 3:15; Ezek 16:11-13; Mal 3:16-18; Mt 13:45-46; 1Tim 2:9; Jam 2:2.

Journey – *Transition:* To go from one place to another; transition; repositioning; the way in the will of God; life; the path we choose to live; movement toward a destination; expedition; trip; one's way; excursion; tour; the road traveled; to reach one's destination.

Reference:Ex 12:37-42; Dt 8;2; Rom 1:10; 15:22-25; Jam 4:13-15; Titus 3:13-14; 3Jn 5-8.

Judge – *Authority:* God; one who administers justice; lawgiver; trial; critic; to determine; resolve; to reach a conclusion; those who judge; judgment; accuser; accuser of the brethren; satan. (Also see Courthouse and Lawyer)

Reference:Ex 18:13-26; Dt 1:16; 16:18; 1Sam 2:25; Isa 2:4; 11:3-4; Jn 12:31; Acts 23:3; 25:9-11; Rom 2:16; 1Pet 1:17; 2:23; 4:5-6.

Jungle: (See Forest)

K

Kangaroo – *To jump:* To jump to conclusions; predisposition; prejudice; to prejudge.

Reference:Pr 18:13; 1Tim 5:21.

Keys – *Authority, power and privilege:* Tools or instruments that give access; to gain entrance, possession or control; solution; explanation; essential for entry; codebook for decryption; entrusted with an important charge; ability to reveal secrets; authority to bind or loose; power to lock or unlock.

Reference:Jdg 3:25; Isa 22:22; Mt 16:19; Lk 11:52; Rev 1:18; 3:7.

Kidneys – *To cleanse:* To clean house; to purify; purification; to rid oneself of waste or impurities.

Reference:Num 17:5; 2Chr 30:18-19; Ps 19:12; 51:2; 73:13; 119:9; Isa 1:24; Ezek 36:25; Zeph 1:18; Eph 5:26.

Kiss – *Affection:* Intimacy; submission to God or to evil; holy love; friendship; the transfer of authority; agreement; covenant; illicit love; the kiss of betrayal or deceit; deception; seduction; friend.

Reference:Gen 33:4; 50;1; 1Sam 10:1; Ps 2:12; Pr 7:13; SS 1:2; Hos 13:2; Lk 15:20; 22:48; Acts 20:37; Rom 16:16; 1Cor 16:20.

Kitchen – *Heart:* Intentions; attitudes; motives; plans; ambitions; passions; what's cooking up on the inside; preparation; service; works; hospitality; provision. (Also see Cafeteria)

Reference:Ps 10:17; 23:5; Pr 16:1; Hos 7:4-7; Mk 15:42; Lk 10:40-42; 23:54; Rom 12:13; 16:23; Eph 6:15; Heb 4:12.

Knees – *Worship (true or false):* Respect; reverence; humility; fasting; prayer; intercession; submission; obedience; point of weakness.

Reference:Gen 33:3; 1Ki 19:18; 2Ki 1:13; Ps 109:24; Isa 35:3; Rom 11:4; 14:11; Php 2:8-11.

Knife – *Words:* Used in consecration; to prune or cut away; wicked and cruel oppressors; stabbing or piercing words; true or false accusations; gossip; sharp rebuke.

Reference:Gen 22:10; Jdg 19:29; Ps 52:2; Pr 30:14; Isa 18:5; Jer 36:23; Titus 1:13.

L

Ladder – *Ascending and/or descending:* To link earth with heaven; to go up or down in position; to climb up or over (to "scale"); to "climb the ladder of success" or "the corporate ladder"; way of escape.

Reference:Gen 11:4; 28:10-19; 2Sam 5:8; Pr 21:22; Jer 5:10; 49:16; Ob 4; Jn 1:51; 3:13.

Lake – *A still body of water:* evangelism (fishing); place of teaching; to look at one's reflection in (as in "mirror-image" in a lake); to examine oneself; a perilous and forbidding place; place of judgment for the wicked (lake of fire); final punishment; death and hell; bottomless pit.

Reference:Lk 5:1-2; 8:22-33; James 1:21-24; Rev 19;20; 20:10; 21:8.

Lamp – *Light:* God; God's Word; enlightenment; guidance; understanding; life; to see or not see; salvation and righteousness; the eyes of man; keeping your lamp lit (wise or foolish virgins); obedience or disobedience to Jesus' teachings; endurance. (Also see Light)

Reference:2Sam 22:29; Job 18:6; Ps 119:105; Pr 6:23; 13:9; Isa 62:1; Mt 6:22-23; 25:1-13; Jn 5:35; 2Pet 1:19; Rev 21:23.

Law – *Rules:* The expressed will of God; mandate; precepts; statues; commandments; rule laid down by a recognized authority; love; to give authority to; charge; requirement; ruling; directive.

Reference:Ex 19:5-6; 1Ki 2:2-4; Ps 119; Lk 16:16-17; Rom 2:14-15; 13:10; Jam 1:25; 1Jn 3:4; 5:3.

Lawyer – *Advocate:* Jesus Christ; defender; counselor; comforter; one who pleads for a cause; to favor; to go to bat for; to support;

to intercede; intercessor; helper. (Also see Courthouse and Judge)

Reference:Mt 22:34-40; Lk 7:30; 14:3-11; Rom 8:26-27; Heb 7:25; 1Jn 2:1.

Prosecuting attorney – *Adversary:* God standing against our enemies; satan; accuser; accuser of the brethren; adversary; devourer; scribe; slanderer; false accuser; proud; self-righteous; to oppose; opposition; one who hinders; foe; enemy.

Reference:Ex 23:22; Num 22:22; 1Ki 5:4; Est 7:6; Ps 74:10; Isa 50:8; Ps 109:6; Mt 5:25; 15:1-2; 1Tim 5:14; 1Pet 5:8; Rev 12:10.

Lead – *Heaviness:* Weight; plumb line; the dross of refining silver; purified by fire.

Reference:Ex 15:10; Num 31:22-23; Ezek 22:18-20; Amos 7:7-8; Zech 5:7-8.

Left – *Spiritual weakness of man:* Rejection; feebleness; handicap; disadvantaged position; not skillful; to walk away from one's calling or purpose; ill warning of future events; unlucky; north.

Reference:Gen 24:49; Judg 3:15,20-21; 20:16; Mt 25:33,41; Jude 6.

Legs – *Strength:* Support; man's walk; to equip; to equip your mind (to "gird up the loins of your mind"); to be prepared; weakness.

Reference:1Ki 18:46; Ps 147:10; Pr 26:7; SS 5:15; Dan 2:33:40; Jn 19:31-33; 1Pet 1:13.

Leopard – *Fear:* Ferocious; swiftness; evil spirit; danger; to lie in wait; cruel; fast; speed, prideful courage; vengeance; powerful leader (good or bad); antichrist; man's inability to change; watcher. (Also see **Cheetah** and **Tiger**)

Reference: Jer 5:6; 13:23; Dan 7:6; Hos 13:7; Hab 1:8; Rev 13:2.

Leviathan (or Crocodile) – *Twisting or coiled:* satan; evil intent; evil spirit; danger; destruction; serpent; crooked; cruelty; pride; false religion; chaos and confusion; disorder; Babylon. (Also see **Alligator** and **Crooked**)

Reference:Job 41:1,10; Ps 74:14; 104:26; Isa 27:1; Jer 51:34; Ezek 29:3; 32:2; Job 41:1,10.

Library – *Knowledge:* Wisdom; understanding; revelation; instruction; teaching; to know; learning; education; study; research; discovery; detection; perverted knowledge.

Reference:Pr 1:7,22,29; 8:10; 29:18; Isa 47:10-14; Rom 1:28; 3:20; 1Cor 8:1; 13:9; Eph 3:3-5; 2Tim 2:15.

Light - *God*: His truth; the Word of God; the glory of God; revealed; exposed; to guide one's way; to reflect; the eyes of man; to illuminate the darkness. (Also see Lamp)

Reference:Ps 18:28; 27:1; 119:105; Eccl 2:13; Isa 49:6; Mt 4:16; 5:14-16; Jn 9:5; 1Tim 6:16; 1Pet 2:9; 1Jn 1:5; Rev 21:23.

Lightning – *Power and majesty of God:* God's wrath; the Second Coming will be like lightning; the arm of God; destruction.

Reference:Ex 9:23; 19:16; 20:18; 2Sam 22:15; Job 36:32; Ps 18:14; Jer 10;13; Mt 24:27.

Lily – *Christ:* Beauty; majesty; spiritual growth; the Father's care for His children; the trumpet call of the Lord. (Also see Rose)

Reference:SS 2:1-2; 5:13; Hos 14:4-5.

Lion – *Kingship:* Jesus Christ; royalty; rulership; dominion; victory; bold; powerful; authority; strength; courage; boldness; satan; antichrist; destroying spirit; roar or yell; ambushing; persecutors; religious tradition.

Reference:Gen 49:9; Num 24:9; Judg 14:18; 1Sam 17:34; 2Sam 17:10; Ps 22:13; 91:13; Pr 28:1; 30:30; Hos 13:7-8; Joel 3:16; 1Pet 5:8; Rev 5:5; 13:2.

Living Room – *Manifest:* Revealed; evident; exposed; mode of living; inner rooms; inner man; without hypocrisy; everyday or current affairs; dwelling. (Also see Porch)

Reference:Dt 29:29; Ps 119:11; Pr 20:27; Mk 2:4-5; Lk 12:1-3; 1Cor 2:10-12; Eph 3:14-19; Col 3:16; 1Tim 6:16; Jam 3:13-18.

Lock – *Restrict:* To protect; to keep out; not accessible; no entry; to seal; unable to open.

Reference:Jdg 3:23-25; Neh 3:13-14; SS 4:12; 5:5; 8:6; Mt 27:66; Lk 11:52; Rev 5:2-9.

Locust - *Devourer:* Potential; possibility; plague; ruin and despair; weakness; promise; develop; change; devastation; destructiveness. (Also see **Butterfly/Caterpillar** and **Grasshopper**)

Reference:Ex 10:13-15; Ps 109:23-24; Pr 30:27; Jer 46:23; Joel 1:4-20; 2:5; Mt 3:4.

M

Magic – Sorcery; witchcraft; astrology; divination; counterfeit miracles; attempt to foretell the unknown through occult means; spells; enchantments; soothsaying; occult practices.

Reference:Num 24:1; Dt 18:10; 2Ki 9:22; Is 47:9; Ezek 13:18-20; Mic 5:12; Acts 19:19.

Magician – *Master of illusion:* Deceiver; to deceive; one who claims understanding and mysteries through magic or the black arts; sorcerer; witch or warlock; astrologist; necromancer; illusionist; false prophet; one who performs counterfeit miracles; the antichrist; one who receives payment for their services.

Reference:Ex 7:11,22; 8:7,18-19; Num 22:7; Dan 1:20; 2:10; Acts 8:9,13:6-8; Acts 19:19; Rev 13:13-18.

Man – *Image of God:* Oneself; messenger (good or evil); angelic or demonic influence; intelligence; stranger; mortal; human race; mankind; sinful.

Reference:Gen 1:26-28; 9:6; Rom 1:23; 1Cor 11:7; 15:49; Col 3:10; Heb 13:2.

Kindly stranger – *Jesus:* One who helps; selfless; charitable; pleasant nature; sympathetic.

Old man – *Mature:* Ancient; elder; age; experienced; wisdom; diminished strength; physical handicaps; sinful nature; old ways; old life; old sin, former conduct.

Reference:Gen 25:8; 1Kin 1:1,15; 12:6-13; Ps 71:9; Ezek 23:43; Lk 1:18; Rom 6:6; Eph 4:22; Col 3:9-10; 1Tim 5:1.

Map – *Direction:* Word of God; guidance; instruction; to plan; strategy; to map out a program; correction; stewardship; light; commandment; the way; the law.

Reference:1Chr 9:24; Pr 6:23; Ezek 1:17; 10:11; Act 7:53.

Manna – *Blessing:* God's provision; sent from heaven; gift; the miraculous; Christ the Bread of Life; bread of heaven; to divinely nourish; God's glory.

Reference:Ex 16:7,14-15; Dt 8:3,16; Ps 78:24-25; Jn 6:30-35; Rev 2:17.

Marriage – *Covenant:* Union or unity; agreement; being equally yoked; joined; marriage supper of the Lamb; Bride = church; Bridegroom = Jesus Christ.

Reference:Gen 2:18-24; Dt 7:3-4; Is 54:5; Joel 2:16; Mt 9:15; 19:4-5; 2Cor 6:14; Eph 5:31-32; Rev 19:7-9; 21:2-9.

Mask – *Concealment:* Disguise; hypocrisy; to cover up; to hide; hidden; secret; to alter or change; to veil from sight; lies and deceit; such as satan disguised as an "angel of light"; test the spirits whether they are from God.

Reference:Num 5:12-13; 1Ki 14:2; 22:30; Job 24:15; 28:21; Ps 40:10; 119:118; Pr 26:24; 27:5; Mt 6:1-2,5,16; 2Cor 11:13-14; 1Jn 4:1.

Mechanic – *Maker:* God; potter; creator; pastor; ministry leader; prophet; counselor; laborer; worker; workmanship; tune-up; in need of adjustment; ministry adjustment; repairer; restorer.

Reference:Ex 31:1-5; 35:30-35; 1Ki 7:13-14; Job 33:26; Ps 23:3; Isa 58:12; Mk 9:12.

Microphone – *Voice:* Preaching; authority; public influence; ministry; ability to speak into people's lives; evangelism.

Reference:Is 61:1; Jon 3:2; Mt 10:27; Mk 16:15; Lk 4:18,43; Act 10:42; 2Tim 4:2.

Milk – *Word of God:* Pure doctrine; foundational truth; teachings; knowledge and understanding of His message; nourishment; spiritual growth; required for mature growth in knowledge and discipleship in the Word of God; the first principles of the Word of God.

Reference:Ex 3:8; Jdg 5:25; Job 10:10; Pr 27:27; 30:33; Isa 28:9; 1Cor 3:2; Heb 5:12-14; 1Pet 2:2.

Mirror – *To see one's reflection:* To examine oneself; to see clearly or dimly; vision; being transformed into the image of Christ; imperfect or distorted reflection; revelation.

Reference:Job 37:18; 1Cor 13:12; 2Cor 3:18; Jam 1:23-25.

Money – *Provision:* Power; wealth; spiritual riches; offering; inheritance; spiritual riches; greed; covetousness; the love of money (root of evil); misuse of; debt.

Reference:Gen 31:14-16; Dt 2:6,28; 14:22-26; 2Ki 5:20-27; Neh 5:2-11; Mt 6:12; 25:27; 1Tim 6:9-11; 2Tim 3:2.

Monkey – *Foolishness:* Mischief; deceitful; not honest (as in "monkey business"); addiction (monkey on your back); wickedness.

Reference:Ps 7:14-16; Pr 24:9; Eph 5:15.

Moon – *Church:* Light in the darkness; Son of Man; night; pagan worship; for signs (in the heavenlies); for seasons, days and years.

Reference:Gen 1:14-16; Dt 4:19; 33:14; Ps 89:37; 104:19; SS 6:10; Isa 30:26; Rev 6:12; 12:1; 21:23.

Bloody moon – *Approaching judgment:*

Reference:Joel 2:31; Acts 2:20; Rev 6:12.

Mortar – *Durability:* Fastening; binding; cement; reinforcing; building; whitewash (as in plaster); building up false hopes; flattery and hypocrisy; foolish.

Reference:Gen 11:3; Ex 1:14; Isa 41:25; Ezek 13:10-16; 22:28; Mt 23:27; Acts 23:3.

Mother – *Nurturing:* Love; kindness; nourishment; provision; comfort; gentle; caregiver; source; heavenly Jerusalem; Israel; protector; ancestry; actual mother.

Reference:Gen 3:20; 17:16; 24:60; 32:11; Ex 2:1-25; 1Ki 1:11-21; Pr 31:1;Isa 66:12-13; Jer 50:12-13; Jn 19:25-27; 1Cor 3:1-2; Gal 4:26; 1Thess 2:7.

Motorcycle – *Person or personal ministry:* Independent; rebellion; pride; loner; self-willed.

Reference:1Sam 15:23; 2Pet 2:10

Mountain – *Great difficulty:* God's presence; a place of worship; protection and refuge; worship (true and false); great joy; faith; overcoming obstacles; judgments; pride; boundaries; obstacles; difficulty.

Reference:Num 34:7-8; Isa 8:18; 27:13; 31:4; 44:23; 65:7; Amos 6:1; Mt 21:21; 24:16; Lk 3:5; 1Cor 13:2.

Mouse or Mice – *Devourer:* Plague; curse; shy; timid (as in "timid as a mouse"); unclean.

Reference:1 Sam 6:4-5; Isa 66:17; Mal 3:11; 2Tim 1:7.

Muddy – *Not clear:* Carnal nature; deception; caused by the flesh; confusion; to make unclear; to blur or obscure; cloudy; to be trampled upon (like mud in the streets).

Reference:Isa 14:23; Ezek 32:13; Mic 7:10

Musketeers – *Soldier:* Warriors; bodyguard; all for one and one for all; unity of the brethren; Christians; vessels of honor; body-guard; loyalty.

Reference:Ps 133:1; Acts 10:7-8; 28:16; Eph 6:13-20; Phil 2:25; 1Tim 6:12; 2Tim 2:3-4,21; 4:7; Phm 2.

N

Nakedness – *Vulnerable:* Exposed; uncovered; truth; honest; of the flesh; self-righteousness; separation from God; shame; wickedness; harlotry; lust; temptation; unprepared.

Reference:Gen 2:19,25; 3:7; Isa 20:3; Ezek 16:36-39; Hos 2:3; Nah 3:4-5; Mic 1:8-11; Mt 25:36-38; Heb 4:13; Jam 2:15; Rev 16:15.

Putting clothes on or changing clothes – *Change:* A changed life; covering; putting on the spiritual covering; covering shame; removal of shame.

Reference:Mk 5:15; Lk 12:28; 2Cor 5:3-4; Gal 3:8; Rev 3:18.

Nation – *The characteristic of the nation:* What are they known for? Industry or reputation; gospel to be preached to; the Great Commission; a people group.

Reference:1Ki 9:7; Mt 24:14; 28:19; Mk 16:15; Lk 4:18; Rom 4:17-18; 1Cor 9:14-24; 2Cor 10:14-16; Rev 2:26.

Neck – *Yoke:* Rescue; bondage; servitude; to force; triumph over a foe; rebel or resist (to stiffen or harden one's neck); stubborn; self-willed.

Reference:Gen 27:40; Dt 31:27; Ps 75:5; Pr 3:22; 29:1; Isa 52:2; Jer 27:12; Hos 11:4; Mt 18:6; Acts 7:51; 15:10.

Necklace – *Beauty:* High position; royalty; pride.

Reference:Gen 41:42; Num 31:50; Ps 73:6; SS 4:9; Dan 5:29.

Net – *To capture:* To catch (as in "fishers of men"); to seek those that are lost; trap, snare; plots of evil men; used by predators; God's wrath; flattery.

Reference:Job 19:6; Ps 9:15; 31:4; Pr 1:17; 29:5; Eccl 9:12; Ezek 12:13; 17:20; Jn 21:6-11.

Night – *Trouble:* Trials; sufferings; distress; death; grave; depravity; ignorance; helplessness, demonic activity (night demon).

Reference:Job 35:10; Ps 77:6; Isa 21:12; 34:14; Mic 3:6; Jn 9:4; 1Thess 5:5.

Nightgown – *Night seasons:* Dreams and visions; to watch for His return; sleep; unprepared; not ready.

Reference:Ps 16:7; 77:2-6; Ezek 11:24-25; Dan 7:1; Zech 1:8; Mk 13:35-37; 2Cor 9:3-4.

North – *God's throne:* Judgment of God; heaven; heavenly; spiritual warfare; scattering winds (north winds); the left hand; to go up; hidden; direction.

Reference:Gen 14:15; Dt 2:3; Job 23:9; 37:9,22; Pr 25:23; Jer 1:13-15.

Nose – *Discernment:* Perception; perceive; recognize; breathing; breath of life; smelling; bondage; enforced obedience; something offensive.

Reference:Gen 7:22; 27:27; 2Ki 19:28; Job 40:24; Isa 37:29; 65:5; Ezek 8:17.

Numbers - Numbers can very often be taken literally and represent a unit of measure, such as units, seconds, minutes, hours, days, weeks, months, years, decades, centuries, etc.

One – *God:* Beginning; first; Genesis; single; only; source; unity; oneness.

Reference:Gen 1:1; 2:24; 8:13; Dt 6:4; Ps 133:1; Isa 44:6; Mt 6:33; 19:6; Jn 3:16; Phil 2:1-2; 1Tim 2:5.

Two – *Judge:* Covenant; agreement; unity; accord; marriage; partnership; testimony; double; double portion; duplicate; couple; witness; twins; divide; division; separate.

Reference:Gen 1:6,8,27; 25:23-26; Dt 17:6; 1Ki 3:25,28; 18:21; 2Ki 2:9; Isa 61:7; Mt 18:16; Jn 8:17,18.

Three – *Godhead:* Trinity; triad; indivisible power; image of God; conform; copy; imitate; obey; divine completeness; likeness; resurrection.

Reference:Gen 1:9-13,26; Ex 19:11; Dt 17:6; Hos 6:1-2; Mt 12:40; 28:19; Lk 13:32; 24:6-7; Rom 8:29; 1Jn 5:6-8.

Four – *Creation:* Worldwide impact; rule and reign; earth or world; four seasons; four corners of the earth (worldwide impact); four winds; kingdom; perfect square (foursquare).

Reference:Gen 1:16-20; 2:10; Lev 11:20-27; Jer 49:36; Ezek 1:8; 37:9; Dan 7:6; Zech 6:5; Mk 13:27; Rev 7:1,2.

Five – *Grace:* Atonement; the cross; redemption; life; five-fold ministry; bread of life; sacrificial service; works; preparation (ten virgins – five wise, five foolish).

Reference:Gen 1:20-23; 41:34; Mt 25:2-20; Mk 6:38-44; 14:16-21; Lk 9:13-16; Eph 4:11.

Six – *Man:* Beast; flesh; humanity; carnal; form; idol; satan's influence.

Reference:Gen 1:26-31; 1Sam 17:4-7; 2Sam 21:20; Lk 1:26; 23:44; Rev 6:12.

Seven – *Perfection:* Completeness; revelation; rest; finished; perfect consecration; holy convocation; fulfillment.

Reference:Gen 2:1-3; Ex 20:10; Lev 8:1-367; 14:7,16,27,51; Num 28:25; Josh 6:4; Acts 6:2-3; Jude 14; Rev 1:4.

Eight – *New beginnings:* Putting off the old and starting new (as in circumcision); cut off; resurrection; restoration; revival; sanctify; death to self; manifest.

Reference:Gen 17:12; Ex 22:30; Num 29:35; Lev 14:10-23; 1Ki 8:66; 2Chr 29:17; Ezek 43:27; Acts 7:8; 9:33; 1Pe 3:18-21; 2Pe 1:14.

Nine – *Fruitfulness:* Fruit; fruits of the Holy Spirit (there are nine fruits of the Spirit); harvest; fullness; maturing; reproduction; gestation; judgment; final.

Reference:Gen 17:1-6; Judg 4:1-3; Lk 15:4-7; 17:17; Rom 6:22; 1Cor 12:1-11; Gal 5:22-23; Heb 13:15.

Ten – *Divine law (Ten Commandments):* Order; government; statutes; commands; trial or test; tribulation; temptation; tithe; responsibility; measure; restoration.

Reference:Ex 20:1-17; 34:28; Lev 27:32; Num 14:22; Dan 5:27; Lk 19:13-25; Acts 25:6; Rev 2:10; 12:3; 13:1; 17:3-16.

Eleven – *End:* Last; finished; shift; transition; shift in leadership or government; change; incomplete; disorganization; disorder; judgment.

Reference:Gen 32:22; 37:9; Ex 26:7; Dt 1:1-8; 1Ki 6:38; 2Ki 9:29; Jer 1:3; Mt 20:6,9,16.

Twelve – *Divine government:* Apostolic fullness; joined; govern; united; God's purposes; oversight.

Reference:Gen 35:23; 49:28; Ex 15:27; 24:4; 28:15-21; Lev 24:5; Est 2:12; Mt 9:20; 19:28; Mk 3:14; Lk 2:42; 6:12-13; 9:1-2; 22:30; Jn 11:9; Acts 6:2-3; 7:8; 19:7; Rev 12:1.

Thirteen – *Rebellion:* Lawlessness; apostasy; backsliding; rejection; revolution; sin; depravity.

Reference:Gen 14:4; 17:25; Est 3:12-13; 8:12-13; 9:1; Jer 25:3.

Fourteen – *Double:* Reproduce; recreate; disciple; service; Passover; liberation of slavery; celebration and gladness; deliverance.

Reference:Gen 31:41; Ex 12:5-8,18; Lev 23:5; Num 9:3-12; 28:16; Josh 5:10; 1Ki 8:65; 2Chr 30;15; 35:1; Ezra 6:19-21; Est 9:15-22; Is 36:1; Ezek 45:21; Mt 1:17; Acts 27:33; Gal 2:1.

Fifteen – *Freedom:* Liberty; valuation (the value of something); honor; sin offering; covered; pardon; holy convocation (Feast of Tabernacle Bread).

Reference:Gen 7:20; Ex 16:1; Lev 23:33-34; 27:7; Nu 28:17; 29:12; 33:3; 2Ki 20:6; Est 9:18-21; Ezek 45:25; Hos 3:2; Gal 1:18.

Twenty – *To judge:* Tried; to govern; to oversee; head of the house; fit or unfit for service; able to go to war.

Reference:Ex 30:14; Num 26:2-4; Jdg 15:20; 16:31; 2Ki 4:42; 1Chr 23:24-28; 2Chr 25:5; 28:1; 31:17; Ezra 3:8.

Twenty-four – *Governmental perfection:* Twenty-four elders around the throne; heavenly rulership; priesthood.

Reference:Rev 4:4-10; 5:8; 11:16; 19:4.

Thirty – *Maturity for ministry:* To begin one's ministry; age of service.

Reference:Num 4:3-46; 2Sam 5:4; Lk 3:23.

Forty – *Generation:* Period of temptation, struggle, and testing; time of spiritual training through trials and difficulty; testing; judgment.

Reference:Gen 7:17; Ex 24:18; Num 14:33; 32:13; Dt 9;25; Ps 95:10; Jon 3:4; Mt 4:2; Lk 4:1-2; Acts 1:3; 7:23,30-42; 13:18; 23:13,21; Heb 3:9,17.

Fifty – *Freedom:* Jubilee; liberty; Pentecost; celebration.

Reference:Lev 25:10-11; Num 8:25; Lk 9:14-17; 16:6.

Seventy – *God's completed purpose:* The days of our lives; accomplished.

Reference:Gen 4:24; Ps 90:10; Isa 23:15-17; Jer 25:11-12; 29:10; Dan 9:2,24; Zech 1:12; Mt 18:22.

One hundred – *Full return:* Full increase; full reward; return on one's seed; inheritance; eternal life.

Reference:Gen 26:12; Mt 13:8,23; 18:12-28; 19:29; Mk 10:30; Lk 8:8.

Six-Six-Six – *The number of the beast:* Antichrist; the number of the man; satan; satan's triad; the dragon; the beast; the false prophet; mark of the beast; lawlessness; control.

Reference:Rev 13:1-18; 16:13.

O

Oak Tree (Terebinth Tree) – *Strength:* Strong; endurance; mighty; stability; place of rest; place of worship; haughtiness; proud and lofty; idolatry (carved images).

Reference:Gen 12:6-7; 13:18; 1Ki 13:14; Is 2:11-13; 44:14-17; Ezek 6:13; Hos 4:13; Amos 2:9.

Ocean – *Mankind:* Nations; the world; perilous and forbidding; troubled lives of the unrighteous. (Also see Sea)

Reference:Dan 7:2-3; Ps 104:24; 107:23-24; 124:4-5; Isa 50:2; 57:20; Hab 2:14; Mt 8:27; 13:47-50; Lk 17:6; Rev 13:1; 21:l.

> **Waves** – *Trouble:* Power; a move of God's Spirit; righteousness; signal or salute; offering; disturbance; tumult; violence; distress; the wrath of God; oppression of the enemy; surge; to rise or fall in activity; upswing; false teachers (raging waves); ungodliness; surrounded and overtaken; death; affliction.
>
> Reference:Ex 29:24-27; Lev 7:30-34; 2Sam 22:5; 2Ki 5:11; Ps 42:7; 65:7; 88:7; 89:9; 107:25-29; 124:4-5; Isa 13:2; 48:18; 57:20; Jon 2:3; Mt 8:23-24; 14:24; Lk 17:6; Acts 27:41; Jas 1:6; Jude 12-13.

Oil – *Anointing:* Holy Spirit.

Olive – *Spiritual fruit:* Fruit of the Holy Spirit; strength and prosperity ("greenness"); anointing; peace; wild = Gentiles; cultivated = Jews.

Reference:Gen 8:11; Ps 52:8; 128:3; Is 17:6; Jer 11:16; Hos 14:6; Hab 3:17; Zech 4:2-12; Rom 11:4,16-25.

Orange (Vermilion) – *Danger:* Fire; color of harvest; harm; loss; injury; hazard; risk; peril; jeopardy; idols; idolatry; unrighteousness; stubbornness; injustice.

Reference:Pr 6:27; Jer 22:14; Ezek 23:14; Mt 5:22.

Orange and black – *Great danger or evil:* Witchcraft; rebellion.

Reference:1Sam 15:23; 2Ki 9:22; 2Chr 33:6; Gal 5:20.

Oven – *Heart:* Intentions; attitudes; motives; passion; intense or hot emotions; testing; judgment.

Reference:Gen 15:17; Lev 2:4; 7:9; 26:26; Ps 21:9; Lam 5:10; Hos 7:4-7; Mal 4:1.

Owl – *Witchcraft:* Wisdom; diplomatic; lonely; emptiness (Isa. 34:11-14); discreet; predator; demonic powers; evil spirits; false prophets; soothsayer; diviner of heresy; fortune-teller; messenger; unclean.

Reference:Lev 11:16-17; Isa 13:21; 34:1-15.

P

Pants – *Operating with authority:* Leadership (wearing the pants in the family); to cover completely.

Park – *Rest:* Recreation; refreshment; delight; leisure; garden; beauty; joy and gladness; to spring forth. (Also Garden)

Reference:Gen 2:8-9; SS 4:12,16; Isa 51:3; 58:11; 61:11; Ezek 36:35; Lk 13:18-19.

Parrot – *Copy:* Imitate; ridicule; mock; resemble; mimic.

Reference:2Kings 2:23; Job 11:3; 12:4.

Passenger – *Ministry worker:* Bondservant; laborer; co-laborer; traveler; self; student; learner; disciple; the person not in control or leading; supporter; assistant; helper; servant; church member; follower; to follow; to be led.

Reference:Ex 24:13; Neh 4:10; Isa 41:8-9; Mt 9:37-38; 11:1; 20:1-8; Rom 16:3-21; 1Cor 3:9; 2Cor 1:24; 8:23; Phil 1:1; 2:25; 1Thes 3:2; 1Tim 5:18; 2Tim 4:11; Phm 1:1,24; Jam 5:4.

Pastor - *Shepherd:* Jesus; one who shepherds a flock; to train and equip the saints for the work of the ministry; to manage; one who governs and nourishes the flock; ruler; to guide; overseer. (Also see Preacher)

Reference:Num 27:17; 1Chr 11:2; Ps 23:1; 28:9; 78:71-72; 80:1; Isa 40:11; 63:11; Jer 2:8; 3:15; 10:21; 17:16; Ezek 34; Mic 7:14; Zech 11:15-17; Mt 9:36; 25:32; Act 20:28; Eph 4:11; Heb 13:20; 1Pet 2:25; 5:2; Rev 7:17.

Pearls- *Wisdom:* Spiritual truths; spiritual wealth; formed within; inner; formed through suffering; price paid; great price; counting the cost; worldly adornment.

Reference:Mt 7:6; 13:45-46; 1Tim 2:9; Rev 17:4; 18:12,16; 21:21.

Pelican – *Lonely:* Unclean; melancholy; inactivity; lives in ruins; dwell in the wilderness. (Also see **Dove** and **Turtledove**)

Reference:Lev 11:18; Dt 14:17; Ps 102:6-7; Isa 34:11; Zeph 2:14.

Pen/pencil – *Tongue:* Words; gossip; communication; agreement; contract; scribe; record.

Penguin – *Formal (as in tuxedo):* Religious spirit; traditional; to pen something; to write; to journal; scribe.

Reference:Est 3:12; Job 19:24; Ps 45:1; 68:34; Isa 8:1; Jer 8:8; 17:1; Hab 2:2; Mt 15:2-6; Mk 7:3-13; Lk 1:63; Gal 1:14; Col 2:8; 2Thes 2:15; 3Jn 1:13.

Pig or Swine – *Loathsome:* False teachers; religious; scoundrel; unclean; selfish; unbeliever; glutton; idolater; ignorance; hypocrite; backslider.

Reference:Dt 14:8; 21:20; Ps 80:13; Ps 23:20-21; Isa 65:4; Mt 7:6; 8:30-32; Lk 15:15-16; 2Tim 3:2-3; 2Pet 2:22.

Pillar – *Support:* Legs; strength; miracles ("pillars of smoke"); God's presence; important person (as in "a pillar in the community"); upright standing; the church of the living God; he who overcomes; angel's feet; assistance.

Reference:Ex 24:4; 33:9-10; Jdg 16:25-29; Job 9:6; SS 5:15; Joel 2:30; Gal 2:9; 1Tim 3:15; Rev 3:12; 10:1.

Pilot – (See Driver)

Pink – *Passion:* Virtue; celibate; innocent; female infant; modest; moral or immoral; flesh; sensual; evil desire.

Reference:Ezek 36:26; Rom 1:26; 7:5; 1Cor 7:9; 12:23; Gal 5:24; Eph 2:3; Col 3:5; 1Thes 4:5; 1Tim 2:9.

Pitch – *Sealing:* To cover; to waterproof; atonement; safety; refuge from judgment (as in Noah's ark); God's judgment; construction.

Reference:Gen 6:14; 14:10; Ex 2:3; Lev 17:11; Isa 34:5-9; Eph 1:1-14; Heb 11:7.

Plow – *Preaching and teaching:* To cultivate the ground; breaking new ground; Christian labor; sowing; affliction.

Reference:Ps 129:1-3; Pr 20:4; Isa 28:24-26; Jer 26:18; Hos 10:11,13; Lk 9:62; 1Cor 9:10.

Police – *Authority:* Governing or spiritual authority; pastor; ministry leader; church leadership; law enforcer; guard; to control; to keep or put in order; public order; safety; rescue; respected.

Reference:Dt 16:18; 1Sam 22:17; 2Ki 11:5-6; 2Chr 19:11; Jer 39:11-14; 40:1-5; Dan 2:14; Mt 5:25; Lk 12:11; 22:4; Acts 4:1-3; 16:35-38; Rom 13:1.

Porch (front) – *Revealed:* Manifest; exposed; gate or entrance; public; open to the world. (Also see Front)

Reference:Ezek 8:16; 41:15; Joel 2:17; Mk 14:68; Jn 5:2; 10:23; Act 3:11; 5:12; 10:17; 12:14.

Pornography – *Sexual immorality:* Works of the flesh; lust; lusts of the flesh; lust of the eyes; idolatry; temptation; adultery in the heart and mind; adultery.

Reference:Gen 3:6; Pr 6:25; Ezek 23:14-18; Mt 4:1-11; 5:27-28; Rom 13:13-14; Gal 5:16-21; 1Pet 2:11; Jude 7; 1Jn 2:16.

Portal – *Gateway:* Entrance; doorway; doorway to heaven; the gates of the New Jerusalem. (Also see Door, Gate/Gateway, or Window)

Reference:Ps 24:7-10; 118:19-20; 141:3; Mic 7:5; Hos 2:15; Rev 3:7-8; 4:1; 21:25.

Post Office – *Communication:* Delivery; letter; correspondence; announce; message; writing; written word; printing; information; sent or received; messenger.

Reference:Gen 32:3,6; Pr 13:17; Isa 18:2; Pr 26:6; Mt 11:10; 25:14; Lk 10:22; Gal 6:11; Phil 2:25; 4:14-18; 1Jn 3:11.

Power Pole – *Power source*: God; Holy Spirit; power of the Holy Spirit; to raise or hold up the source of power; high position of authority over others; one that has control or authority; to supply with power; ability to function; plugged in; ability to effect; physical might; energy to do work; strength; brawn; muscle.

Reference:Job 36:22; Ps 59:16; 111:6; 147:5; Isa 40:29; Mic 3:8; Nah 1:3; Lk 4:14; 24:49; Act 1:8; 1Cor 7:37; Eph 3:20; Php 1:19; 4:19; 2Tim 1:7-8; Rev 2:26.

Preacher – *Messenger:* One who proclaims the gospel; public proclamation; to cause one to hear; pastor; teacher; evangelist; spiritual authority (good or bad); satan; deception; false preacher; false teacher. (Also see Pastor)

Reference:Eccl 1:2; 12:9-10; Isa 61:1-2; Jer 23:1; Jon 3:2; Mk 16:20; Rom 10:14; 2Cor 11:4-13; 1Tim 2:7; 2Tim 1:11; 2Pet 2:5.

Pregnant – *Birthing:* To be called; conception; beginning; to conceive; to sow; to produce; the process and time of development; expectant; in process; anticipation; desire.

Reference:Gen 21:2; Jer 1:5; Hos 9:11; Mt 24:19; Gal 1:15; 1Thes 5:3; Heb 11:11; Jam 1:15.

Labor pains – *Trials:* Sudden destruction; the inevitable; pain and sorrow.

Reference:Ps 48:6; Is 13:8; 26:17; Mic 5:3; Jn 16:21; 1Thes 5:3.

Miscarriage – *Loss:* Abort; unjust judgment; failure; repentance.

Prison – *Captivity:* Bondage; bound; prisoner; ensnared; snare; confinement for prisoners; slavery; lawlessness; rebellion; stubborn; hard labor; torture. (Also see Bird Cage, Cage, and Dungeon)

Reference:Jdg 16:21-25; Jer 5:26-27; 52:11; Ezek 19:9; Lk 4:18; Acts 22:24-25; Heb 2:15.

Prisoner – *Sinner:* Persecuted saints; spiritual darkness; punishment; exile; banishment; bondage; oppressed; unsaved; stubborn; rebellious; sufferings.

Reference:Jdg 16:21; Job 3:18; Ps 137:3-5; 146:7; Isa 49:9; Jer 38:6; Zech 9:11-12; Acts 12:4; 2Tim 2:25-26.

Prophet – *Prophetic word:* Divine revelation; future event; divine guidance; prophetic gift; actual prophet; warning; correction; rebuke; false prophet; deception.

Reference:Dt 13:1-4; 18:18-22; Isa 44:26; Ezek 3:17; Joel 2:28; Mt 7:15; 24:11-24; Lk 6:26; 2Tim 3:16.

Prostitute (Harlot) – *Spiritual adultery:* Seduction; adultery; temptation; shameless; works of the flesh; idolatry; snare.

Reference:Lev 19:29; 20:5-6; Josh 2:1; Judg 2:17; Pr 5:3-20; Isa 57:3-9; Jer 3:3; Hos 4:12-15; Gal 5:19; Rev 17:1-18.

Purple – *Royalty:* Majesty; kingship; royalty; rule; reign; authority; noble; riches; wealth; sacred; luxury; false authority; prosperity.

Reference:Jdg 8:26; Est 8:15; SS 3:10; 7:5; Dan 5:7,16,29; Mk 15:17; Lk 16:19; Rev 17:4.

QR

Queen – *To rule with the king:* Wife of the king; president, pastor, or the one in charge; crowned; counsels the king; Jezebel; to exert influence (good or bad) in public affairs.

Reference:1Ki 11:19; Est 1:9; 5:3; Dan 5:10-12; Rev 2:20; 18:7.

Rabbit – *Increase:* Multiplication; growth; fast growth; reproductive.

Reference:Gen 1:22,28; Ps 67:6; 107:38; Pr 20:21; Isa 9:3; Jer 29:6; 30:19; Jn 3:30; Act 16:5; 1Cor 3:6-7; 2Cor 9:10; Heb 6:14; 1Thes 3:12; 4:10.

Raccoon – *Mischief:* Deceitful; rascal; thief; bandit; outlaw; plunderer; robber.

Reference:Ps 7:14-16; 62:10; Isa 42:24; Ezek 7:22; Hos 6:9; 7:1; Amos 3:10; Oba 1:5; Jn 10:1; 18:40.

Raft – *Powerless:* Without direction; to be tossed to and fro; aimless conduct; adrift; to be operating under your own power.

Reference:Ps 88:5; Eph 4:14; 1Pet 1:18

Rags – *Filthiness:* Iniquity; unclean; unrighteousness; self-righteousness; drowsiness.

Reference:Job 15:16; Pr 23:21; 30:12; Isa 64:6; Ezek 22:15; Zech 3:3-5; 2Cor 7:1; Jam 1:21; 2:2-4; 1Jn 1:7-10; Rev 22:11.

Rain – *Teaching:* Wisdom; revival; restoration; refreshing; life; Word of God; blessing; depression; trial; disappointment (to "rain on someone's parade"); heavenly provision and blessing; God's judgment and wrath.

Reference:Dt 11:11-15; 32:2; Job 20:23; 29:23; Isa 55:10-11; Jer 3:3; Zech 10:1; Mt 7:27; Heb 2:7; Jam 5:7,17-18.

Rainbow – *Covenant with God:* Promise; sign of love and hope; God's faithfulness and mercy; the glory of the Lord; the presence of God; is a reflection from the storm itself; connected with God's judgment of the world.

Reference:Gen 9:13-17; Ezek 1:28; Rev 4:3; 10:1.

Rape – *To violate:* To abuse; to take advantage of; murder; to force an issue; without consent or approval; deception; unlawful; lawlessness.

Reference:2Sam 13:12-15; Deut 22:25-26

Rat – *Betrayal:* Mean person; plague; devourer; unfaithful; double-cross; sell out; stab in the back (as in forty pieces of silver); unclean.

Reference:1Chr 12:17; Mal 3:11; Mt 10:4; 26:45; Jn 18:2.

Red – *Sin:* Atonement; fire; life (blood), the essential element of atonement; selfish; covetous; passionate life; persecution; drunkenness; anger; war; judgment; suffering; violence; bloodshed; lust; enthusiasm; zeal; death, satan.

Reference:Gen 9:4-6; 25:25,30; 2Ki 3:22-23; Ps 75:8; Pr 23:29-32; Isa 1:18; 63:2; Nah 2:3; Zech 1:8-15; Heb 9:22; Jam 4:1; Rev 6:4; 12:3.

Ribs – *To roof over:* To cover; protect; protective; woman's creation.

Reference:Gen 2:21-22; Job 40:18; Dan 7:5; Hos 13:8.

Right – *Rightness:* Righteousness; authority; power; the power of God revealed through man; natural; accepted; certainty; to be straight; truth; trustworthiness; success; advantage; south.

Reference:Gen 48:18; Ex 15:6; 1Sam 24:17; Mt 5:29-30; 25:33; Act 7:55-56; Eph 6:1; Jam 5:16; 1Pet 3:12,22; 1Jn 3:7.

Ring – *Authority:* Position; social status; ownership.

Reference:Gen 41:42; Est 3:12; Pr 11:22; Lk 15:22; Jam 2:2.

Signet ring – *Authority:* Ownership; to seal something.

Reference:Gen 38:18; 41:42; Ex 28:11; Neh 9:38; Est 3:12; 8:8; Dan 6:17; Hag 2:23.

River – *The Holy Spirit:* Jesus, the King; Spirit of life (living waters); bathing or cleansing; baptism (by water and by the Spirit); healing; irrigation and provision; peace; blessing of God; God's delights; peace; life; refreshing; revival; tears; to be overwhelmed or overcome. (Also Stream)

Reference:Gen 2:10-14; Ex 2:5; 2Ki 5:10; Ps 1:3; 36:8-9; 46:4; 124:4; Is 32:1-2; 48:18; 66:12; Lam 3:48; Mt 3:6; Jn 7:38-39; Rev 22:1-2.

Muddy or turbulent river – *Trouble:* Turbulent situation; difficult circumstances; overwhelmed or overcome; grief; tears; sin; wickedness; wilderness; unstable; destruction.

Reference:Ps 89:9; 119:136-143; 124:4; Ps 138:7; Isa 14:23; 26:16; 57:20; Lam 3:48; Ezek 32:13.

Road – *The way (good or bad):* Jesus Christ; the way of salvation; path; highway; highway of holiness; the call or commission of the gospel; narrow and difficult; broad and destructive; destiny or destination.

Reference:Num 20:17; 21:22-23; Deut 3:1; Pr 15:19; 16:17; Is 11:16; 35:8-10; 40:3; 51:10; 62:10; Jer 18;15; 31:21; Mt 7:13-14; Jn 14:6; Acts 8:26.

Muddy road – *Flesh:* The way of man; lusts of the flesh; temptation; the slippery way; to be stuck in the mud; weakness; unrighteousness.

Reference:Job 30:19; Ps 69:2,14; Is 10:6; 57:20; Jer 38:6; Zech 9:3; 2Pet 2:22.

Robe: (See Coat)

Rock – *The church's foundation:* Jesus Christ; salvation; refuge; protection; the foundation of faith; a stone of stumbling and a rock of offense; permanence; cornerstone; strength; integrity; stability.

Reference:Deut 32:4-18; 1Sam 13:6; Job 19:24; Ps 31:2-3; 89:26; 94:22; Is 8:14; 32:2; Mt 7:24-25; 16:18; 1Cor 10:4; Eph 2:20.

Roller Coaster – *Fast:* Speedy; instability; emotionally unstable; switchback; highs and lows; unfaithfulness; wavering; depression; trials; amusement; excitement; to twist.

Reference:Ps 82:5; Pr 5:6; Isa 40:4; Jas 1:6-8; 2Pet 3:16

Roof – *Covering:* Shelter; hospitality; mind; thoughts; shield; lid; protection.

Reference:Gen 19:8; 2Sam 11:2; Mt 8:8; 10:27.

Rooftop grass – *Humiliation for the wicked:* Short-lived; momentary prosperity; ruin; the destruction of the enemy; dismayed and confounded.

Reference:2Ki 19:26; Ps 129:6; Isa 37:27.

Rooster (Cock) – *Arise and shine:* Watch; alert; to make aware of; attentive; signal; SOS; proud; arrogant; display; look; wake up; be ready and alert; leader (as in "to rule the roost").

Reference:Mt 26:34; Mk 13:35; 14:30.

Root – *Source of life and nourishment:* Jesus Christ, the Messiah; to provide stability and nourishment; established; to cause to bear fruit; remnant; spiritual life; spiritual foundation (rooted in love); the source of evil (money); bitterness; heart of wickedness.

Reference:2Ki 19:30; Ps 80:9; Pr 12:3,12; Isa 11:1,10; Jer 12:2; Hos 14:5; Mt 13:6,21; Lk 8:13; Rom 11:16-18; Eph 3:17; Heb 12:15; Rev 22:16.

Rose – *Christ:* Romance; love; courtship; passion; fragrance; restoration. (Also see Lily).

Reference:SS 2:1; Isa 35:1.

Running – *Striving:* Eagerness (in evil or good); working out your salvation; confidence; swiftness; to contend; to go without restraint; administrative activity; operating; to oversee an activity.

Reference:Job 9:25; Ps 119:32; Pr 1:16; Jer 12:5; 1Cor 9:24-26; Gal 2:2; Php 2:16; 2Thes 3:1; Heb 12:1.

Rust – *Corruption:* Decay; destruction; destruction of earthly treasures; corrosion; a witness against the wicked; scum and filthiness; lewdness.

Reference:Gen 6:11-12; Dt 13:13; Ps 14:1-3; Ezek 16:47; 24:11-13; Mt 6:19-20; 2Cor 7:2; Eph 4:22; Jam 5:3.

S

Sackcloth – *Repentance:* Mourning; to lament; grieve; weeping; prayer and supplication; lament; humility; penitence; sorrow for sins or offenses.

Reference:Gen 37:34; Est 4:1-4; Job 16:15; Ps 30:11; 69:11; Isa 22:12; Dan 9:3; Joel 1:13; Mt 11:21; Rev 11:3.

Salt – *Preservative or seasoning:* Purifying; everlasting covenant of friendship and faithfulness; being a good influence; peace; wise speech; barrenness and desolation.

Reference:Num 18:19; Dt 29:23; Jdg 9:45; 2Ki 2:20-21; Job 6:6; Mt 5:13; Mk 9:49-50; Col 4:6; Jam 3:12.

Sand – *Multitude:* Descendants; all future generations; children of Israel; innumerable; shifting foundation; instability; not firm; weakness; cannot be measured or counted; generations.

Reference:Gen 22:17; Isa 10:22; Hos 1:10; Mt 7:26; Rom 9:27; Heb 11:12; Rev 20:8.

Scarlet – *Blood atonement:* Sacrifice; Christ; royalty; cleansing; purification; covering; separation; brilliance, brightness; prosperity; agreement; sacred; sin; death; blasphemy and abomination; filthiness and fornication.

Reference:Gen 38:28-30; Ex 12:7; Lev 14:4; Num 4:8; 19:6; Josh 2:18,21; 2Sam 1:24; Isa 1:18; Mt 27:28; Heb 9:19; Rev 17:3-4.

School – *Education:* Learning; teaching; instruction; discipleship; knowledge; learning in the home; the church; training; equipping; study; intellectual; teaching ministry; teacher.

Reference:Lev 10:11; Dt 6:6-10; 1Chr 25:7-8; Pr 19:20,27; 22:6; Isa 50:4; Lk 2:46; 6:40; Act 19:9; Eph 4:12; 2Tim 3:15-16; Heb 12:11.

Scorpion – *Stinging words:* Accusation; deception; destruction; danger; painful; satanic; agents of antichrist; witchcraft; sting of death (sin).

Reference:Dt 8:15; Ezek 2:6; Lk 10:19; 11:12; 1Cor 15:56; Rev 9:3,5,10.

Sea – *The human race:* The seething nations of the world; a perilous and forbidding place; troubled lives of the unrighteous; the extension of the gospel; turbulent; dangerous; evil, chaos; boundary. (Also see Ocean)

Reference:Job 26:12; Ps 89:9; 107:23-30; Isa 11:9; Jer 5:22; Dan 7:2; Mt 13:47; Rev 13:1; 21:1.

Sea of Glass – *Holiness and purity:* Like crystal; righteous living; clarity; revelation.

Reference:Ezek 1:22-28; Rev 4:6; 15:2.

Seat: (See Chair)

Seed – *Word of God:* Tithe, faith; offspring, remnant, sons and heirs of Jesus Christ, divine nature of God, Jesus, gospel message.

Reference:Gen 21:12-13; Isa 6:13; 53:10; Mt 13:37-38; Lk 8:11; Jn 7:42; Rom 1:3; 2Cor 9:10; Gal 3:16,26-29; 1Jn 3:9.

Seraphim – *Angels of fire:* Ministers of fire; burning or glowing ones; agents of purification; attendants of God; ones of praise; communicator between heaven and earth; six wings – two to fly with, two to cover their face (humility), and two to cover their feet (respect).

Reference:Ps 104:4; Is 6:2-7; Heb 1:7.

Sex or Intercourse – *Agreement:* Unity; union; becoming one; immorality; perversion; stumbling blocks.

Reference:Ps 133:1; Act 15:20,29; Rom 1:29; 1Cor 5:9-11; 1Thess 4:3; Rev 2:14-21; 22:15.

Shadow – *Shelter:* Protection; cast from an object which intercepts the light rays; evidence of time (sundial); not permanent; healing source; fleeting; death; darkness; gloom or despair; representation of something; to follow or trail; to follow in someone's footsteps; phantom or ghost.

Reference:Jdg 9:36; 2Ki 20:9-11; Job 14:2; Ps 91:1; 102:11; Eccl 6:12; Isa 32:2; Mt 4:16; Acts 5:15; Col 2:17; Heb 10;1; Jam 1:17.

Shark – *Greedy:* Crafty; cunning; deceitful; self-serving; self-willed; artful; danger; vicious; malicious; savage disposition.

Reference:Job 5:12; 15:5; Ps 83:3; Pr 1:19; 15:27; 21:26; Ezek 22:12; Rom 1:29; Eph 4:19; 2Pet 2:10.

Shed: (See Barn and Store)

Sheep – *Christ:* The redeemed; saints; church; innocent; defenseless; vulnerable; unsaved people. (Also see **Cattle, Goats**, and **Ram**)

Reference:2Sam 24:17; Ps 79:13; 95:7; 100:3; Mic 5:8; Mt 10:6; 25:33; 26:31-34; Jn 1:29; 10:1-27; Acts 8:32; 20:28; Heb 13:20; 1Pet 2:25.

Lamb – *Jesus Christ:* Redeemer; King; innocent; humility; those who follow Jesus Christ; sacrifice; atoning; life-giving.

Reference:Isa 53:7; Jn 1:29; 1Pet 1:19; Rev 5:6-13; 7:9-14; 15:3.

Ship – *Church or large ministry:* Ministry of evangelism (fishers of men); carrier of supplies or cargo; able to withstand the fierce storm; sturdy.

Reference:Ps 107:23; Pr 31:14; Jon 1:5; Acts 27:37-38; Jam 3:4; Rev 8:9; 18:19.

Shipwreck: (See **Airplane Crash** and **Car Crash**)

Shoes (Sandals) – *Readiness:* Preparation for service; alertness; to make or get ready; to think ahead; ready with the gospel of peace; walk; protection for walking.

Reference:Ex 12:11; Deut 29:5; Josh 9:5,13; Isa 5:27; Eph 6:15; 2Tim 4:2; Titus 3:1.

Boots – *Hard work:* Difficult tasks; protection for the walk; soldier or warrior; war; feet strengthened for conquest.

Reference:Ps 18:33-38; Isa 9:5; Mic 4:13.

Taking off shoes (sandals) – *Reverence:* Honor; respect; to regard; devotion; to appreciate deeply; not prepared; not ready.

Reference:Ex 3:5; Josh 5:15; Jn 13:5-6; Act 7:33.

Shoes that don't fit – *Not equipped for service:* Walking in something you're not equipped for; operating outside your calling; preparation; unworthiness. (Also see Apparel/ Clothes that don't fit)

Reference:2Ki 24:16; 1Chr 12:23; Pr 24:27; Jn 1:27; 2Tim 3:16-17.

Shopping Center (Market) – *Public:* Business dealings; revenue; merchandise; hiring of laborers; profit; buying and selling; public discussions; publicity.

Reference:Isa 23:3; Ezek 27:9,15,24; Mt 20:3; Mk 7:4; Acts 16:19; 17:17; 1Cor 10:25.

Shorts – *To cut short:* Brief; falling short of the glory of God; not long; to shame; weakened strength.

Reference:Ps 89:45-47; 102:23-27; Isa 59:1-2; Mic 6:10; Rom 3:23; 9:28; 1Cor 1:7; 7:29; Heb 4:1; 12:14-15; Rev 12:12.

Shoulder – *To bear:* Burden bearing; to take responsibility; support; hold; stubborn; disobedience; rebellion; bondage; yoke; servitude; authority; rulership.

Reference:Gen 21:14; 24:45-46; Neh 9:29; Job 31:35-36; Ps 81:6; Isa 9:4-6; 22:22; Mt 23:4; Lk 15:5.

Sign – *An indication:* Distinguishing mark; a miracle which points to Jesus Christ; representations of divine power.

Reference:Gen 9:12-17; Josh 4:6-7; Isa 19:19-20; Mt 12:38-39; 24:30; Mk 3:15; Lk 11:16; 1Cor 1:22; 2Thess 3:17.

Silver – *Redemption:* The Word of God; knowledge; understanding; revelation knowledge; God's refined people; wealth.

Reference:Gen 13:2; Ps 12:6; 66:10; Pr 2:3-4; 3:13-14; 1Cor 3:12-14; Col 2:3; 2Tim 2:20.

Sister – *Blood relative:* Spiritual sister (in the Lord); self; female relationship; comparable to brotherly relationship; female relative; women of the same tribe; servant of the church; the church; someone she reminds you of; family; actual sister.

Reference:Gen 24:30-60; Num 25:18; Mt 12:48-50; Rom 16:1; 1Cor 7:15; 2Jn 1:13.

Skin – *Flesh:* Sinful human nature; fragile; weakness; covering; deception; lust; desire; sin.

Reference:Gen 3:21; 27:16; Ex 26:14; 29:14; Mk 14:38; Rom 8:1-13; Gal 5:19-21; Eph 2:3,11,15.

Slipping - *Yielding to temptation:* To make a mistake; to fall off from a standard or level; calamity.

Reference:Dt 32:35; 2Sam 22:37; Job 12:5; Ps 17:5; 26:1; 38:16; 73:2; 94:18.

Sloth – *Laziness:* Slow moving; sluggishness; sleepy; decay; poverty.

Reference:Pr 18:9; 19:15,24; 20:4; Eccl 10:18.

Smoke – *Prayers of the saints:* The presence of God; destruction; distress; the end of the world; sacrificial burnt offering – the smoke was the offering which ascended up to God; God's holy anger (from His nostrils); signs and wonders of the Holy Spirit; plague; the torment of the bottomless pit.

Reference:Gen 19:28; Ex 19:18; 20:18; 2Sam 22:9; Ps 119:83; Isa 6:4; 51:6; Hos 13:3; Acts 2:19; Rev 8:4; 9:2-3; 14:11; 15:8.

Sofa: (See **Couch**)

Snail – *Slow:* Sluggard; withdrawal; retreat; protective, foolish.

Reference:Gen 33:14; Ex 4:10; Ps 58:8; Pr 14:29; Lk 24:25; Act 27:7; Jas 1:19.

Snake (Serpent) – *Deception:* Subtle; cursed; slander; gossip; back-biting; false accusations; false prophecies; beguile; crooked; demon; danger; critical spirit; satan; slander; witchcraft; wickedness; intoxication; malice; divination; enemy; sin; a forked tongue. (Also see **Dragon** and **Leviathan**)

Reference:Gen 3:1-15; Ps 58:3-4; 140:3; Pr 23:31-32; Isa 14:29; 27:1; Jer 46:22; Mic 7:17; 2Cor 11:3; Rev 20:2.

Asp – *Man's evil nature:* False teacher.

Reference:Dt 32:33; Job 20:1-16; Ps 140:3; Isa 11:8; Rom 3:13.

Cobra – *Deception:* Poisonous words; to bewitch or charm; to deceive.

Reference:Josh 17:2; Ps 58:4; 91:13; Isa 11:8.

Fangs – D*anger:* Threat; intentions of evil.

Reference:Job 29:17; Ps 35:16; 58:6; Pr 21:6; 30:14; Lam 2:16; Joel 1:6; Amos 5:19; Acts 7:54.

Lizard – *Deception:* Lying; long tale; unclean; false prophet; diviner; divination; deceiver.

Reference:Lev 11:29-30; Dt 18:14; Isa 9:14-15; 32:7; Jer 27:9; 29:8; Ezek 22:28; Zech 10:2; Eph 4:25.

Rattler – *Loose words:* Warning; threat; alarm; loose words.

Reference:Ps 140:3; Jer 4:19; 49:2; Ezek 3:21; 33:4-5.

Snow – *Purity:* Cleansing power; cleanness; to be white or pure; spotless; brilliancy; the effective power of God's Word.

Reference:Job 9:30; Ps 51:7; Pr 25:13; Isa 1:18; 55:10; Lam 4:7; Dan 7:9; Mt 28:3; Rev 1:14.

Dirty snow - *Not pure:* Dirty, mixed; adulterated; foul; contaminated; polluted; unclean; sin; corruption.

Reference:Pr 25:26; Zeph 3:1-4; Rom 8:20-21; 2Pet 2:20.

Soap – *Cleansing:* Purification; to clean; to wash; cleansed of our iniquity; repentance; to make ready.

Reference:Job 9:30; Jer 2:22; Mal 3:2.

Socks – *Not prepared:* Not completely ready.

Reference:Ex 3:5; Josh 5:15; Eph 6:15.

Soldier – *Christians:* Christian workers; obedience; devotion; spiritual armor; national military; service; fighter; war; warfare; spiritual warfare; subduing riots; guard; protection; persecution; enemy; violence; accuser; opponent.

Reference:Mt 8:9; Lk 3:14; Acts 10:7; 12:4-6; 21:31-35; Eph 6:10-18; Phil 2:25; 2Tim 2:3-4.

Son: (See Children/One's Own Children)

South – *World:* Temptation; sin; trial; whirlwind; south wind; chamber; lips; flesh; deception; corruption; place of refreshment; to go down; at the right hand.

Reference:Gen 12:9; Josh 10:40; Job 37:9; Ps 126:4; SS 4:16; Acts 27:13; 28:13.

Sparrow – *Care:* Value; small; comparatively worthless; providence.

Reference:Ps 84:3; 102:7; Pr 26:2; Mt 10:29-31; Lk 12:6-7.

Spider – *Sin:* Wickedness; deception; false doctrine; temptation; evil; occult; demonic attack; witchcraft.

Reference:Job 8:14; Pr 30:24,28; Eccl 7:26; Rom 6:16.

Black widow – *Danger:* Deadly; slander; demonic attack; occult; witchcraft.

Reference:Jam 3:8.

Web – *Trap or snare:* Lies; deceit; demonic network; witchcraft.

Reference:Job 8:14; Eccl 7:26; Isa 59:5.

Square – *Legalism:* Religiousness; religious traditions; strict; sticking to out-of-date ideas; unprogressive; old-fashioned; conservative; conventional; excessive conformity to the law; foursquare; just; fair; balanced.

Reference:Act 17:22; Jam 1:26.

Staff (or Rod)– *Leadership:* Authority; shepherding; military weapon; government; rod of discipline and correction; Jesus; the rule of Christ; God's protection of believers.

Reference:Ex 4:17; 9:23; 1Sam 17:7; Ps 2:9; 23:4; 89:32; Pr 13:24; Isa 11:1; 14:5; Mt 10:10; Mk 6:8.

Stairs (or Steps) – *Increase or decrease:* Promotion or demotion; ascending or descending; spiritual process; procedure.

Reference:Gen 28:12; Ex 20:26; 2Ki 9:13; Job 18:7; 23:11; 31:4,37; Ps 40:2; 44:18; Pr 5:5; 14:15; 30:4; Ezek 40:22-49; Jn 5:7; Eph 4:8-10; 1Pet 2:21; Rev 7:2; 21:10.

Upstairs – *Increase:* Incline; spiritual incline; to ascend; prayer; prosperity; excel; thoughts (righteous or carnal). (Also see Attic, Elevator/Top Floor, Up/Upstairs, and Upper Room)

Reference:Ps 24:3; 68:18; Jn 3:13; Act 1:13-14; 20:7-8; Rev 7:2.

Downstairs – *Demotion:* Moral decline; to descend; to go down; spiritual decline; backsliding; stubborn; faithless; old life of sin and idolatry; failure.

Reference:Josh 10:11; 2Chr 28:19; Pr 7:27; 14:14; Jer 3:6-22; 8:5; 31:22.

Stars – *Person:* Messiah; Christ (as the "Morning Star"); generations; princes; rulers; nobles of the earth; leader or role model; hero or movie star; brightness; idolatry; astrology; sign.

Reference:Gen 37:9-10; Num 24:17; Isa 14:12-13; Dan 8:10; 12:3; Jude 1:13; Rev 6:13; 8:10-12; 9:1; 12:4; 22:16.

Stone – *Headship (chief cornerstone):* Christ (the Rock); Christ as foundation; Christians; memorial; altar; permanent; strength; firmness; a sure foundation; memorial; members of the church = living stones; building; hardness; insensitivity; idolatry.

Reference:Gen 28:18-22; 31:45; 35:14; 49:24; Ex 4:25; 24:12; Lev 26:1; Josh 4:9,20; 1Sam 7:12; 25:37; Ps 118:22; Isa 8:14; 28:16; 57:6; Ezek 11:19; 36:26; Zech 7:12; Mk 13:1-2; Acts 4:11; 1Pet 2:4-8.

Precious stones – *Value:* Beauty; durability.

Reference:SS 5:14-15; Isa 54:11-12; Lam 4:7; Rev 4:3; 21:11,21.

Store – *Storehouse (barns):* Treasury; provision; supply; equip. (Also see Barn)

Reference:Dt 28:5-8,17; 1Chr 27:25; Ps 33:7; Pr 3:10; Jer 50:26; Joel 1:17; Mal 3:10.

Stork – *Affection:* Nesting; expectant; delivery; new birth; new experience; new baby; upcoming event; appointed times; unclean.

Reference:Lev 11:19; Dt 14:18; Ps 104:17; Jer 8:7.

Storm – *Wrath:* Trouble; distress; trials or tribulations; to wander in the wilderness; oppression; affliction; difficulty; sorrow; separated (as in "chaff in the wind"). (Also see **Whirlwind**)

Reference:Job 21:18; Ps 107:23-43; 148:8; Isa 25:4; 28:2; Nah 1:3.

Straight – *Righteousness:* Not wandering; proper or straight course; justice; honest; upright; correct order; unmixed; undiluted.

Reference:Ps 5:8; Pr 4:25; 9:15; Eccl 1:15; 7:13; Isa 40:3-4; Jer 31:9,39; Mt 3:3; Lk 3:4-5; Jn 1:23; Heb 12:13.

Straw: (See Crops/Straw)

Stream: (See River)

Sulfur: (See Brimstone)

Sun – *Light:* Illumination; glory; happiness; clear; day; light (opposite of darkness); daylight; God; the light of God; morning; for signs (in the heavenlies).

Reference:Gen 1:3; Ps 27:1; 56:13; 84:11; 89:15; Pr 16:15; Isa 5:20,30; 9:2; 30:26; Mic 7:8-9; Eph 5:8-14; 1Thess 5:5; 2Tim 1:8-10; 1Jn 5:7; 2:8-10.

Swimming – *Moving in the Holy Spirit:* Moved or led by the Holy Spirit; going deep or deeper in the Spirit; stepping out in faith; operating in faith.

Reference:Ezek 47:5; Lk 4:1; Act 10:38-47; 15:8; Rom 8:14; 1Cor 2:10; Gal 3:5; 5:5-25.

Not able to swim – *Not able to move in the Spirit:* Not filled with the Spirit; not operating in faith; to quench the Holy Spirit.

Reference:1Thes 5:19; 2Pet 3:17.

Swimsuit – *Operating in the Spirit:* prepared and ready to go deep in the Spirit.

Reference:Jn 21:7.

Speedo – *To go fast:* Swiftness; rapid; to move fluidly; how fast something is going; ability to move quickly.

Reference:Ps 31:2; 69:17; 143:7; Isa 5:19-26; Jn 21:7.

Sword: (See Armor/Sword)

T

Table – *God's provision:* Fellowship; intimate relationship; hospitality; serving; preparation; altar (for showbread), a symbol of the heart tablet; agreement; money changing; business transaction; to conduct business.

Reference:Ex 39:36; 1Ki 2:7; Ps 23:5; Pr 3:3; Isa 21:5; 28:8; Jer 17;1; Mal 1:7,12; Mt 21:12; Mk 11:15; Lk 7:37; 22:27-30; Jn 2:15; Acts 6:2; Rom 2:15; 1Cor 10:21.

Tail – *To do harm:* Stinging; rump; end; behind; to trail behind; beneath; not the lender but the one who borrows; false prophet.

Reference:Ex 4:4; Dt 28:13,44; Jdg 15:4; Isa 9:14-15; Rev 9:10,19; 12:4.

Wagging tail – *To flatter:* Agreeable; to move; remove; quake; shake; stir; to agitate; to disturb; fooled by flattery; to blaspheme (wagging their heads).

Reference:Jer 18:16; Lam 2:15; Dan 11:32; Mt 27:39-40; Mk 15:29-30.

Tares – *Troublemaker:* False teachers; false seed; harmful; inferior; sown by the enemy (satan); sons of wickedness; lawlessness; sown by the devil. (Also Weed)

Reference:Job 31:40; Zeph 2:9; Mt 13:25-40.

Tears – *Prayers:* To beseech or entreat; intercession; to appeal or implore; affliction; anguish; mourning; to grieve; repentance; trials.

Reference:2Ki 20:5; Est 8:3; Ps 6:6; 39:12; 42:3; 56:8; 80:5; 116:8; 126:5; Isa 38:5; Lam 2:11,18; Mal 2:13; Lk 7:38; Acts 20:19; 2Cor 2:4; Rev 7:17.

Teeth – *Wisdom:* Understanding; persecution; words; judgment; to devour; to consume.

Reference:Ps 37:16; 57:4; 58:6; 124:6; Pr 30:14; Isa 41:15; Dan 7:5-7; Zech 9:7-8; Lk 13:28; Rev 9:8.

Dentures – *Conversion:* To replace what was lost; gained wisdom and knowledge from experiences; restoration; replacement; replacing false wisdom for the truth.

Reference:Act 3:19; Rom 5:3-5.

Eyetooth – *Revelation:* Vision; foresight; envision; something revealed; enlightening; divine disclosure.

Reference:Ps 32:8; Isa 29:18; Rom 16:25; 1Cor 1:7; 14:26; 2Cor 12:17; Gal 1:12; Eph 3:3; 1Pet 1:13.

Gnashing of teeth – *Futility of the wicked:* Anger; hatred; scorn; contempt; to mock; verbal abuse.

Reference:Job 16:9; Ps 35:16; Lam 2:15-16; Mt 13:42,50; Lk 13:28; Acts 7:54.

Wisdom teeth – *Wisdom:* Understanding; divine understanding; knowledge; insight; good sense; judgment.

Reference:Ex 31:3; Ps 37:30; 49:3; Pr 10:13-31; Lk 21:15; Act 6:10; 1Cor 2:1-13.

Termites – *Corruption:* Destruction; hidden or secret sin; evil spirit.

Reference:Ps 11:3; Hab 1:6.

Thief – *Deception:* To steal; one who steals; secrecy; to come unexpectedly; deceiver; fraud; trick; satan; evil intentions; hidden; to steal, kill, and destroy.

Reference:Gen 31:19-35; Ex 20:15; Pr 29:24; Jer 2:26; 49:9; Hos 7:1; Joel 2:9; Mt 24:43; Lk 12:39; Jn 10:1,10; 12:6; Rom 2:21; 13:9; Eph 4:28; Col 2:8.

Thigh – *Promise or oath:* Truth; strength; shame humiliation; sorrow (to strike the thigh).

Reference:Gen 24:2-9; 32:24-32; 47:29; Ps 45:3-4; SS 3:8; Isa 47:2; Jer 31:19; Ezek 21:12; Rev 19:16.

Threshing Floor – *Separate:* To divide; God's judgment; the labor of ministry; to sift out wickedness.

Reference:Ruth 3:2-14; Pr 20:26; Isa 41:14; Jer 51:33; Hos 9:1-2; 13:3; Joel 2:24; Mic 4:12; Mt 3:12; 1Cor 9:9-10.

Thunder – *God's voice:* Sound; powerful; divine power; divine displeasure with God's people; vengeance.

Reference:Ex 9:23; 1Sam 2:10; 12:17; Job 37:2-5; Ps 18:13; 29:3-4; 77:18; Isa 30:30.

Tiger - *Stubborn:* Stalker; methodical in one's attack; predator; stealth; to trap or snare (as in "the love of money"); deception; to lie in wait; false witness; camouflaged or hidden; dangerous; wild or hard to deal with; devourer; threat; difficult to tame; territorial; one who dwells in the wilderness; Antichrist. (Also see **Cat** and **Leopard**)

Reference:1Ki 13:18; Ps 27:12; 91:3; SS 4:8; Jer 13:23; Ezek 14:15-16; Hos 13:7; Hab 1:8; Mt 22:16; Mk 14:1; 1Tim 6:9; Rev 13:2.

Tin – *Dross:* Purification; scum; waste; worthless; matter; refuse.

Reference:Num 31:22; Ezek 22:17-20.

Tongue – *Speech:* Praying in the Holy Spirit; spiritual gift; people; race; words; the source which reveals the heart; source of trouble; source of fire; world of iniquity; arrows; bows; deceit.

Reference:Ex 4:10; 2Sam 23:2; Ps 15:3-4; 34:13; 35:23; 64:3-8; 109:2; Pr 10:20; 21:23; Isa 66:18; Act 2:26; 1Cor 12:28-30; 14:2-27; Phil 2:11; Jam 1:26; 3:5-8; 1Pet 3:10; Jude 20; Rev 5:9; 13:7.

Tornado: (See **Whirlwind**)

Tractor – *Powerful work:* Hard work; great power; slow but powerful; to cultivate and prepare the soil; ability to accomplish what other people and ministries cannot; powered by the Holy Spirit; to plant; harvester; reaper.

Reference:Act 1:8; 4:33.

Train – *The church or ministry:* Discipleship; to be able to move many people down a path or road; powerful ministry; connected line of people or ministry; people or ministries working in connection with each other; unity of the faith; equipping of the saints; to influence growth as desired; to teach through instruction; disciple; tutor; coach; teach; to train and equip for ministry; to prepare or become prepared; to direct; to impart knowledge; to come into alignment; to follow behind; trail; favor and wealth (lower hem of a garment).

Reference:Ps 25; 144:1; Pr 22:6; Isa 6:1; Hos 10:11; 11:1-4; Lk 6:40; Eph 4:11-13; 6:4; Heb 12:7; 2Pet 2:14.

Train tracks - *Path:*Discipleship path, way of holiness, route, trail, a course laid out, awareness of a fact or progression.

Tree – *Righteous:* Individuals; saints; Jesus Christ; leader; eternal life; kingdoms of prosperity; idolatry.

Reference:Gen 1:11-12; 2Ki 17:10; Ps 1:3; 37:35; 52:8; 92:12; Pr 3:18; 11:30; 13:12; Isa 44:14,17; Ezek 17:24; Mt 7:17-20; Rev 22:2,14.

Olive tree (or oil tree) – *Kingship:* Peace; Israel; the righteous; the true church; fruit of the Spirit; witnesses; anointed; fuel for lamps.

Reference:Gen 8:11; Lev 2:1; Jdg 9:8-9; Ps 52:8; Isa 17:6; 41:19; Jer 11:16; Zech 4:11-14; Rom 11:17,24; Rev 11:3-4.

Palm tree – *Righteous:* Upright; victory.

Reference:Ps 92:12; Jer 10:5; Joel 1:12; Jn 12:13; Rev 7:9-10.

Tunnel – *Underground passageway:* Way of access; way of escape; to go through or under; transition; trial; water channel; channel for transport; conduit; aqueduct.

Reference:2Sam 5:8; 22:16; 2Ki 18:17; 20:20; 2Chr 32:30; Job 28:10; 38:25; Isa 7:3; 27:12; 36:2; Ezek 31:4.

Turbulent: Causing disturbance through violence, agitation, or tumult; rage; the voice of the enemy; tempest; the judgment of the Lord.

Reference:2Ki 19:28; Job 27:20; 39:7; Ps 65:7; 74:23; 83:2; Isa 28:2; 33:3; 37:29; Mt 8:24; Act 27:18.

Turkey – *Lack of judgment:* Foolish; dumb; thanksgiving.

Reference:Lev 22:29; Ps 50:14; 100:4; 107:22; 73:22; Eccl 9:12; 2Cor 4:15; 9:11; Phil 4:6; 1Tim 4:4.

Turn Around – *Change direction:* Spiritual change; reverse action; change course; to turn a corner; transform; heart change; convert; to turn from evil; revolution; shift; revert; return; to turn towards evil.

Reference:Ex 14:5; 23:2; 1Sam 10:6,9; Ps 4:2; 6:10; 18:37; 21:12; 40:4; 56:9; 80:18; 90:3; 119:37,39,51,79,157; Pr 4:27; 7:25; Lam 5:14; Lk 1:16-17; Act 28:27; Heb 12:25; 1Pet 3:11; 2Pet 2:21.

Turtle (or Tortoise) – *Slow:* To move with difficulty; dawdler; slowpoke; slow-moving; sacrifice; gentle; withdrawal; retreat; protective; timidity; to hide from.

Reference:Gen 33:14; Ex 4:10 2Sam 11:15; Job 9:13; 36:7; Ps 74:11; Lk 24:25; Act 27:7; 2Tim 1:7; Jam 1:19.

Turtledove – *Affection:* Offering of the poor; gentle nature; peace; love; forgiveness; innocence; Holy Spirit; forgiveness; the church. (Also see **Dove** and **Pelican**)

Reference:Lev 12:2, 6-8; Ps 74:19; SS 2:11-12; Jer 8:7; Mt 3:16; Mk 1:10; Lk 2:24; 3:22.

UV

Up – *Ascension:* Spiritual ascension; self-glorification; pride; increase; exalted; high above; lofty; loftiness.

Reference:Gen 13:1; Josh 4:14; Ps 24:3; 68:18; 97:9; 108:5; Pr 16:18; 30:13; Isa 2:2-4,11,17; Lk 1:52; Eph 4:8-10.

Upstairs – *Increase:* Incline; spiritual incline; prayer; upper room; prosperity; excel; thoughts (righteous or carnal). (Also see Attic, Elevator/Top Floor, and Stairs/Upstairs)

Reference:Gen 49:26; Jn 3:30; Acts 1:13-14; 20:7-8; 1Cor 14:12; 1Thess 3:12.

Upper Room: (See Attic, Elevator/Top floor, Stairs/Upstairs, and Up/Upstairs)

Vehicle – *Ministry:* The church is Christ's vehicle to reach the world; a means of transporting people or goods to their desired destination; means of getting from one point to another; vessel; method; to carry.

Reference:Gen 45:19; 1Sam 6:8-14; 2Sam 6:3; 1Chr 13:7; Amos 2:13; Mt 28:19-20.

Veil – *To conceal:* To obscure from view; covering; to separate; Christ's flesh sacrificed for us; access or hindered access into God's presence (Also see Curtain)

Reference:Gen 24:65; Ex 40:3; SS 4:1; Isa 25:7; 47:2; Mt 27:51; 2Cor 3:13-16; Heb 6:19; 9:3; 10:20.

Virgin – *Purity:* Innocent; spotless; no stain; modest; unspoiled; undefiled; wise or foolish; untouched sexually; chaste; Israel; mother of Jesus.

Reference:Lev 21:14; Isa 37:22; Jer 31:4; Mt 25:1-13; 1Cor 7:28-38; 2Cor 11:2; Rev 14:4.

Vulture – *Greedy:* Unclean; covetous; ravenous; scavenger; stalker; devourer. (Also see **Buzzard**)

Reference:Lev 11:13-14; Dt 14:12-13; Job 28:7; Pr 30:17; Isa 34:15; Jer 12:9.

W

Walking – *Working out your salvation:* Conduct in life (Enoch and Noah "walked with God"); demeanor; course of action; unbelief (as in "to walk in darkness"); holy and happy (as in "to walk in the light"); faith; carnal desires (as in "to walk according to the flesh"); Spirit-led (as in "walk in the Spirit"); wisdom.

Reference:Gen 13:17; Ex 18:20; Dt 5:33; 1Ki 2:3-4; Ps 23:4; 116:9; 119:35,45; Mic 2:11; Hab 3:19; Jn 8:12; Rom 8:1-4; 2Cor 5:7; Gal 5:16,25; 5:16-25; Eph 5:2-8; Col 1:10; 2:6; 3:5-7; 4:5; 2Pet 2:10; 1Jn 1:6-7; 2Jn 1:6.

Walls – *Defense:* Barrier; protection; division; separation; to divide; to surround; salvation; defensive. (Also see Fence)

Reference:Neh 4:3; Ps 62:3; 122:7; Isa 2:15; 26:1; 30:13; 60:18; Amos 1:7-14; Zeph 1:16; Zech 2:4-5; Acts 23:3; Eph 2:14.

Warfare – *Spiritual battles:* War against the powers of darkness; entangled with worldly pleasures; military force; battle between good and evil.

Reference:Isa 40:2; Jer 49:2; Rom 8:38-39; 1Cor 16:13; 2Cor 10:4; Eph 6:12; 1Tim 1:18; 2Tim 2:4; Jam 4:1-4; 1Pet 5:8.

Wasps: (See Bees)

Water – *Word of the Lord:* Jesus Christ; spiritual growth; teaching; knowledge; refreshing; peace; eternal life; to quench one's thirst; regeneration; cleansing; purification; baptism; sanctification; salvation; life-giving; irrigating.

Reference:Gen 18:4; Ex 19:10; 40:7-32; Ps 1:3; 23:2; Isa 12:3; 55:1; Ezek 47:1-12; Jn 4:10-15; 7:37-38; Acts 8:36-39; Eph 5:26; Rev 22:17.

Waves: (See Ocean/Waves)

Weapon – *Offensive or defensive tool:* Armor; spiritual tools for combat; tools of warfare; used in attack; used to overcome one's adversary; to arm and ready oneself with protection; indignation.

Reference:Dt 1:41; 1Chr 12:37; Neh 4:17; Isa 13:5; 54:17; Jer 21:4; 22:7; 50:25; 51:20; Ezek 9:1; 2Cor 10:4-6; Eph 6:11-17; 1Jn 5:4.

Weasel – *Evading:* Hedge; dodge; wicked; going back on a promise; tattletale; betrayer (Judas); traitor.

Reference:1Chr 12:17; Isa 16:3; Mk 14:10; 2Tim 3:2-7.

Wedding Dress – *The bride of Christ:* Purity; righteousness; holiness; ready; covenant; commitment; the union of Christ with the church.

Reference:Ps 45:13-15; Isa 49:18; 61:10; Jer 2:32; Joel 2:16; Rev 21:2.

Wedding Ring – *Covenant:* Promise; fidelity; adoption into a family.

Reference:Gen 41:42; Lk 15:22.

Weeds: (See Tares)

Well – *Source:* Water of life; refreshment; revival.

West – *Behind:* End; sunset; going down; grace; last; conformed; death.

Reference:Ex 10:19; Dt 11:24; Ps 103:12; Isa 59:19; Lk 12:54.

Wheat: (See Crops/Wheat)

Wheel – *Momentum:* Motion; movement; moving power; spiritual activity; rotate; revolve; turning; to pivot; whirl; to roll; transport; speed; threshing instrument; God's throne; a potter's wheel.

Reference:Pr 20:26; Eccl 12:6; Jer 18:2-8; Ezek 1:15-16; 10:1-22; 11:22.

Wife – *Companion:* Helpmeet; actual wife (she may represent herself); covenant; agreement; marriage; God's relationship with Israel; the bride of Christ; church; faithful or unfaithful; someone or something you are devoted to (business, job, hobby, etc).

Reference:Gen 2:18,24; Pr 5:15-17,20; 31:11-12; Isa 54:5-6; 62:4-5; Jer 3:1; Hos 2:16-20; Mal 2:14-15; Jn 4:17-18; 1Cor 7:1-5, 33; 2Cor 11:2; Eph 5:23,32; Heb 13:4; Rev 19:7; 21:2.

Whirlwind (or Tornado/Hurricane) – *To toss:* Snatch away; destruction; the fury of the Lord; to scatter; overtaking the wicked; twisting; confusion; distortion; an unexpected turn.

Reference:2Ki 2:1,11; Job 37:9; Ps 58:9; Pr 1:27; 10:25; Jer 30:23; Hos 8:7; Zech 7:14.

White – *Purity:* Without mixture; light; Christ; holiness; spotless; righteousness; salvation; the saints; blameless; ripe (for harvest); innocence; glory and majesty; triumph; sacred.

Reference:2Ki 5:27; Ps 68:14; Dan 7:9; Zech 6:3; Mt 17:2; 28:3; Jn 4:35; 20:12; Rev 3:4-5; 6:2; 7:9; 15:6; 19:8,11.

White Elephant: (See Elephant)

Wilderness – *Desert:* Wandering; testing; desolation; lacking sustenance; parched and bare; unfruitful; sterility; solitude; rebellion; temptation; persecution; unbelief.

Reference:Gen 14:6; 16:7; Ex 3:1; 5:1; Num 14:29; Dt 8:2; 32:10; Job 24:5; Ps 65:12; 68:7; Isa 27:10; 33:9; Joel 2:3; Mt 12:43; Lk 11:24.

Wind – *Breath:* Spirit of life; to toss; wavering; indecisive; separate (as in "chaff in the wind"); Holy Spirit; power of the invisible God; windy words = empty words; what you can feel but not see.

Reference:Gen 7:21-22; Ex 15:10; Num 11:31-32; Job 4:9; 7:7; 21:18; 27:21-23; Ps 33:6; Mt 7:25; Eph 4:14; Jam 1:6; Jude 12.

Window – *Access:* Opening; entrance; "windows of heaven"; storehouses of blessing; way of escape; window of opportunity; porthole. (Also see Door)

Reference:Gen 7:11; Josh 2:15-21; 1Sam 19:12; Pr 7:6; SS 2:9; Mal 3:10; 2Cor 11:33.

Wings – *Protection and defense:* Extremity; strong and loving care; mercy; spiritual transport; healing; deliverance (Ex 19:4); covering (Ex 25:20); protection; carried (Deut 32:11); flying; swiftness; unlimited ability.

Reference:2Sam 22:11; Ps 55:6; 57:1; 68:13; Isa 40:31; Mal 4:2; Mt 23:37.

Winter – *Season of cold:* Darkness; lack; barren; waiting; to hibernate; stagnate; difficulty; harshness; tribulation.

Reference:Gen 8:22; Ps 74:17; Pr 20:4; SS 2:11; Mt 24:20; Mk 13:18; Acts 27:12; 2Tim 4:21.

Witch or Warlock – *Witchcraft:* Sorcerer; evil intentions; divination; rebellion; suppressor; works of the flesh; control; deception; fraud; false prophets; evil influence; enemy; evil spirit; spiritual warfare.

Reference:Ex 22:18; Dt 18:10-12; 1Sam 15:23; 28:3-25; 2Ki 9:22; 21:6; Jer 14:14; Ezek 13:6-7; Acts 13:6-8; Gal 5:19-21.

Wolf – *Devourer:* False prophet; satan; evil leader; womanizer; philanderer; danger; terror; ferocious; ravenous; bloodthirsty. (Also see **Cougar**)

Reference:Gen 49:27; Isa 11:6; 65:25; Ezek 22:27; Jer 5:6; Mt 7:15; 10:16; Lk 10:3; Jn 10:12; Acts 20:29.

Fangs – *Danger:* Evil intentions; the wicked; to gnash one's teeth.

Reference:Job 29:17; Ps 35:16; 58:6; Pr 30:14; Lam 2:16; Joel 1:6; Acts 7:54.

Woman – *Helper:* Glory of man; bride of Christ; the church; beautiful; a weak or helpless man; the context of the woman will help determine who she represents; yourself (she can represent yourself); the church.

Reference:Gen 2:18-23; 34:3-12; Isa 3:12; 19:16; 62:5; 1Cor 11:3-15.

Old woman – *Mature:* Ancient; elder; age; experienced; wisdom; mentor; diminished strength; physical handicaps; sinful nature; lacking sexual desire.

Reference:Gen 25:8; 1Kin 1:1,15; 12:6-13; Ps 71:9; Ezek 23:43; Lk 1:18.

Wood – *Perishable:* Contentious man; humanity; idolatry; worthless doctrine; yoke; works of the hands.

Reference:Pr 26:20-21; Eccl 10:9; Isa 30:33; Jer 10:8; 28:13; Dan 5:4,23; 1Cor 3:12; Rev 9:20.

Work Clothes – *Works of the ministry:* Occupational works; workmanship; to work hard; what one does for a living; profession; calling; career; toil; labor; task; job; employment; workaholic; busy work.

Reference:Pr 14:23; Isa 49:4; Eccl 2:11; 1Cor 3:9-17; 1Thess 1:3; 2:9; 4:11.

Wormwood – *Calamity:* Bitter experience; idolatry; adultery; God's judgment.

Reference:Dt 29:18; Pr 5:4; Jer 9:15; Amos 5:7; Rev 8:10-11.

XY

Yard – *Life experience:* Possession; participation in life; pertaining to life's situations; events; life; discover; familiarity.

Reference:Lk 8:14; 21:34; Jn 4:5; Act 26:4-5; 28:7; 1Cor 6:3-4; 1Tim 2:2.

Backyard – *Past or previous:* Experience or event; memory; remember; recollection; learned from experience; old sins; what is behind; to turn back; to turn back to evil.

Reference:Ps 7:12; 18:37; 44:10,18; 77:6; 78:57; 126:1-4; Eccl 1:11; 2:16; Jer 24:6; Ezek 23:21; Mt 11:12; Mk 13:16; Lk 10:13; 17:31; Heb 10:38-39; 2Tim 1:5; Jam 5:19; 2Pet 1:9.

Front yard – *Present or future:* Prophetic; current; immediate; what is ahead; plans; main entrance; confront; goal.

Reference:Pr 6:18; 16:9; 20:18; Jer 29:11; Lk 18:29-30; Act 20:24; 1Cor 9:24; 2Cor 1:17; Heb 12:1; Rev 1:19.

Yellow (Golden) – *Gift:* Joy; hope; bright; majesty; anointed; honor; marriage; family; friendship (as in a yellow rose); coward; fear; timid; deceit.

Reference:Job 37:22; Ps 68:13; Zech 4:12; 2Tim 1:7.

Yoke – *Burden:* Oppression; legalistic ordinances; marriage; submission; working together; united in position; covenant union; discipleship; joined; servant; service; labor; bondage to sin; binding; burden; harness; control; slavery.

Reference:Dt 28:48; 1Ki 12:4-14; Jer 27:8; Lam 1:14; Mt 11:29-30; Lk 14:19; Acts 15:10; 2Cor 6:14; Gal 5:1; 1Tim 6:1.

Z

Zebra – *Mixture:* Intermarriage of different races; unity of all races; black and white; double-minded; mixing of righteousness and lawlessness; a horse of a different color; rare; uncommon; unusual; seldom seen.

Reference:Gen 30:35-37; Ps 12:2; 119:113; Isa 1:22; Zech 9:6; Mt 5:36-37; 19:6; Acts 17:26; Jam 1:8; 4:8.

Zoo – *Public display:* Exhibit; show; behavior; strange; creation.

Reference:Gen 1:20-25; Zech 9:6; Mt 1:19; Lk 5:26; Col 2:15; Jam 3:16.

The
Dreamer's
JOURNAL

Unlocking your dreams using biblical truths

Date of Dream: _____

Dreamer: _____

Title: _____

Dream Purpose:_____

DREAM:

_____
_____
_____
_____
_____
_____
_____
_____
_____
_____

WORD DEFINITIONS:

_____
_____
_____
_____
_____
_____
_____
_____
_____

SHORT INTERPRETATION:

_____
_____
_____
_____
_____

SCRIPTURE REFERENCE:

LONG INTERPRETATION:

SCRIPTURE REFERENCE:

MY CONCLUSION & RESPONSE:

_____
_____
_____
_____
_____

As for these four young men, God gave them knowledge and skill in all literature and wisdom; and Daniel had understanding in all visions and dreams.

Daniel 1:17

Date of Dream: _____

Dreamer: _____

Title: _____

Dream Purpose: _____

DREAM:

_____
_____
_____
_____
_____
_____
_____
_____
_____
_____

WORD DEFINITIONS:

_____
_____
_____
_____
_____
_____

_____
_____
_____

SHORT INTERPRETATION:

_____
_____
_____
_____
_____

SCRIPTURE REFERENCE:

_____
_____
_____

LONG INTERPRETATION:

_____
_____
_____
_____
_____
_____
_____
_____
_____
_____
_____
_____
_____
_____
_____
_____
_____
_____
_____

_____
_____

SCRIPTURE REFERENCE:

_____
_____
_____
_____
_____
_____

MY CONCLUSION & RESPONSE:

_____
_____
_____
_____
_____

Inasmuch as an excellent spirit, knowledge, understanding, interpreting dreams, solving riddles, and explaining enigmas were found in this Daniel, whom the king named Belteshazzar, now let Daniel be called, and he will give the interpretation.

Daniel 5:12

Date of Dream: _____
Dreamer: _____
Title: _____
Dream Purpose:_____

DREAM:

_____
_____
_____
_____

_____
_____
_____
_____
_____
_____

WORD DEFINITIONS:

_____
_____
_____
_____
_____
_____
_____
_____
_____

SHORT INTERPRETATION:

_____
_____
_____
_____
_____

SCRIPTURE REFERENCE:

_____
_____
_____

LONG INTERPRETATION:

_____
_____
_____

_____

_____

_____

_____

_____

_____

_____

_____

_____

_____

_____

_____

_____

_____

_____

_____

_____

SCRIPTURE REFERENCE:

_____

_____

_____

_____

_____

_____

MY CONCLUSION & RESPONSE:

_____

_____

_____

_____

_____

Then the Angel of God spoke to me in a dream, saying, "Jacob." And I said, "Here I am."

Genesis 31:11

Date of Dream: _____

Dreamer: _____

Title: _____

Dream Purpose: _____

DREAM:

_____
_____
_____
_____
_____
_____
_____
_____
_____
_____
_____

WORD DEFINITIONS:

_____
_____
_____
_____
_____
_____
_____
_____
_____

SHORT INTERPRETATION:

_____
_____

SCRIPTURE REFERENCE:

LONG INTERPRETATION:

SCRIPTURE REFERENCE:

_____

_____

_____

MY CONCLUSION & RESPONSE:

_____

_____

_____

_____

_____

And they said to him, "We each have had a dream, and there is no interpreter of it." So Joseph said to them, "Do not interpretations belong to God? Tell them to me, please."

Genesis 40:8

Date of Dream: _____

Dreamer: _____

Title: _____

Dream Purpose: _____

DREAM:

_____

_____

_____

_____

_____

_____

_____

_____

_____

_____

WORD DEFINITIONS:

_____
_____
_____
_____
_____
_____
_____
_____
_____

SHORT INTERPRETATION:

_____
_____
_____
_____

SCRIPTURE REFERENCE:

_____
_____
_____

LONG INTERPRETATION:

_____
_____
_____
_____
_____
_____
_____
_____
_____
_____

_____
_____
_____
_____
_____
_____
_____
_____
_____

SCRIPTURE REFERENCE:

_____
_____
_____
_____
_____

MY CONCLUSION & RESPONSE:

_____
_____
_____
_____
_____

And so it was, when Gideon heard the telling of the dream and its interpretation, that he worshiped. He returned to the camp of Israel, and said, "Arise, for the LORD has delivered the camp of Midian into your hand."

Judges 7:15

Date of Dream: _____
Dreamer: _____
Title: _____
Dream Purpose: _____

DREAM:

_____

_____

_____

_____

_____

_____

_____

_____

_____

_____

WORD DEFINITIONS:

_____

_____

_____

_____

_____

_____

_____

_____

SHORT INTERPRETATION:

_____

_____

_____

_____

SCRIPTURE REFERENCE:

_____

_____

_____

LONG INTERPRETATION:

_____

_____

_____

_____

_____

_____

_____

_____

_____

_____

_____

_____

_____

_____

_____

_____

_____

_____

_____

_____

SCRIPTURE REFERENCE:

_____

_____

_____

_____

_____

MY CONCLUSION & RESPONSE:

_____

_____

_____

_____
_____

When the LORD brought back the captivity of Zion, we were like those who dream. Then our mouth was filled with laughter, and our tongue with singing. Then they said among the nations, "The LORD has done great things for them."
Psalm 126:1-2

Date of Dream: _____
Dreamer: _____
Title: _____
Dream Purpose: _____

DREAM:
_____
_____
_____
_____
_____
_____
_____
_____
_____
_____

WORD DEFINITIONS:
_____
_____
_____
_____
_____
_____
_____
_____
_____

SHORT INTERPRETATION:

_____

_____

_____

_____

_____

SCRIPTURE REFERENCE:

_____

_____

_____

LONG INTERPRETATION:

_____

_____

_____

_____

_____

_____

_____

_____

_____

_____

_____

_____

_____

_____

_____

_____

_____

_____

_____

_____

SCRIPTURE REFERENCE:

_____
_____
_____
_____
_____
_____

MY CONCLUSION & RESPONSE:

_____
_____
_____
_____
_____

"The prophet who has a dream, let him tell a dream; and he who has My word, let him speak My word faithfully. What is the chaff to the wheat?" says the LORD. "Is not My word like a fire?" says the LORD, "and like a hammer that breaks the rock in pieces?"

Jeremiah 23:28-29

Date of Dream: _____
Dreamer: _____
Title: _____
Dream Purpose: _____

DREAM:

_____
_____
_____
_____
_____
_____
_____
_____

_____
_____

WORD DEFINITIONS:

_____
_____
_____
_____
_____
_____
_____
_____

SHORT INTERPRETATION:

_____
_____
_____
_____

SCRIPTURE REFERENCE:

_____
_____
_____

LONG INTERPRETATION:

_____
_____
_____
_____
_____
_____

_____

_____
_____
_____
_____
_____
_____
_____
_____
_____
_____
_____
_____
_____
_____

SCRIPTURE REFERENCE:

_____
_____
_____
_____
_____
_____

MY CONCLUSION & RESPONSE:

_____
_____
_____
_____
_____

He sought God in the days of Zechariah, who had under-standing in the visions of God; and as long as he sought the LORD, God made him prosper.

2 Chronicles 26:5

Date of Dream: _____

Dreamer: _____

Title: _____

Dream Purpose: _____

DREAM:

_____
_____
_____
_____
_____
_____
_____
_____
_____
_____

WORD DEFINITIONS:

_____
_____
_____
_____
_____
_____
_____
_____
_____

SHORT INTERPRETATION:

_____
_____
_____
_____
_____

SCRIPTURE REFERENCE:

_____
_____
_____

LONG INTERPRETATION:

_____
_____
_____
_____
_____
_____
_____
_____
_____
_____
_____
_____
_____
_____
_____
_____
_____
_____
_____

SCRIPTURE REFERENCE:

_____
_____
_____
_____
_____

MY CONCLUSION & RESPONSE:

_____
_____
_____
_____
_____

*He stretched out the form of a hand, and took me by a lock
of my hair; and the Spirit lifted me up between earth and
heaven, and brought me in visions of God to Jerusalem, to
the door of the north gate of the inner court, where the seat
of the image of jealousy was, which provokes to jealousy.
And behold, the glory of the God of Israel was there, like the
vision that I saw in the plain.*

Ezekiel 8:3

Date of Dream: _____
Dreamer: _____
Title: _____
Dream Purpose: _____

DREAM:

_____
_____
_____
_____
_____
_____
_____
_____
_____
_____

WORD DEFINITIONS:

_____
_____

_____
_____
_____
_____
_____
_____
_____
_____

SHORT INTERPRETATION:

_____
_____
_____
_____
_____

SCRIPTURE REFERENCE:

_____
_____
_____

LONG INTERPRETATION:

_____
_____
_____
_____
_____
_____
_____
_____
_____
_____
_____
_____
_____
_____

_____

_____

_____

_____

_____

_____

SCRIPTURE REFERENCE:

_____

_____

_____

_____

_____

MY CONCLUSION & RESPONSE:

_____

_____

_____

_____

_____

In the first year of Belshazzar king of Babylon, Daniel had a dream and visions of his head while on his bed. Then he wrote down the dream, telling the main facts.

Daniel 7:1

Date of Dream: _____

Dreamer: _____

Title: _____

Dream Purpose: _____

DREAM:

_____

_____

_____
_____
_____
_____
_____
_____
_____
_____
_____

WORD DEFINITIONS:

_____
_____
_____
_____
_____
_____
_____
_____
_____

SHORT INTERPRETATION:

_____
_____
_____
_____

SCRIPTURE REFERENCE:

_____
_____
_____

LONG INTERPRETATION:

_____
_____
_____
_____
_____
_____
_____
_____
_____
_____
_____
_____
_____
_____
_____
_____
_____
_____
_____
_____
_____
_____

SCRIPTURE REFERENCE:

_____
_____
_____
_____
_____
_____

MY CONCLUSION & RESPONSE:

_____
_____
_____

_____

_____

I have also spoken by the prophets, and have multiplied visions; I have given symbols through the witness of the prophets.

Hosea 12:9

Date of Dream: _____

Dreamer: _____

Title: _____

Dream Purpose: _____

DREAM:

_____

_____

_____

_____

_____

_____

_____

_____

_____

WORD DEFINITIONS:

_____

_____

_____

_____

_____

_____

_____

SHORT INTERPRETATION:

_____

_____

_____

_____

_____

SCRIPTURE REFERENCE:

_____

_____

_____

LONG INTERPRETATION:

_____

_____

_____

_____

_____

_____

_____

_____

_____

_____

_____

_____

_____

_____

_____

_____

_____

_____

_____

SCRIPTURE REFERENCE:

_____
_____
_____
_____
_____
_____

MY CONCLUSION & RESPONSE:

_____
_____
_____
_____
_____

It is doubtless not profitable for me to boast. I will come to visions and revelations of the Lord: I know a man in Christ who fourteen years ago—whether in the body I do not know, or whether out of the body I do not know, God knows—such a one was caught up to the third heaven. And I know such a man—whether in the body or out of the body I do not know, God knows— how he was caught up into Paradise and heard inexpressible words, which it is not lawful for a man to utter. Of such a one I will boast; yet of myself I will not boast, except in my infirmities. For though I might desire to boast, I will not be a fool; for I will speak the truth. But I refrain, lest anyone should think of me above what he sees me to be or hears from me.

1 Corinthians 12:1-6

Printed in the United States
202497BV00001B/136-1524/P